New Directions for
Student Services

Elizabeth J. Whitt
EDITOR-IN-CHIEF

John H. Schuh
ASSOCIATE EDITOR

D1121028

Strategic Planning in Student Affairs

Shannon E. Ellis

EDITOR

Number 132 • Winter 2010
Jossey-Bass
San Francisco

STRATEGIC PLANNING IN STUDENT AFFAIRS
Shannon E. Ellis (ed.)
New Directions for Student Services, no. 132
Elizabeth J. Whitt, Editor-in-Chief
John H. Schuh, Associate Editor

NEW DIRECTIONS FOR STUDENT SERVICES (ISSN 0164-7970, e-ISSN 1536-0695) is part of The Jossey-Bass Higher and Adult Education Series and is published quarterly by Wiley Subscription Services, Inc., A Wiley Company, at Jossey-Bass, 989 Market Street, San Francisco, California 94103-1741. Periodicals Postage Paid at San Francisco, California, and at additional mailing offices. POSTMASTER: Send address changes to New Directions for Student Services, Jossey-Bass, 989 Market Street, San Francisco, CA 94103-1741.

New Directions for Student Services is indexed in CIJE: Current Index to Journals in Education (ERIC), Contents Pages in Education (T&F), Current Abstracts (EBSCO), Education Index/Abstracts (H.W. Wilson), Educational Research Abstracts Online (T&F), ERIC Database (Education Resources Information Center), and Higher Education Abstracts (Claremont Graduate University).

Microfilm copies of issues and articles are available in 16mm and 35mm, as well as microfiche in 105mm, through University Microfilms Inc., 300 North Zeeb Road, Ann Arbor, Michigan 48106-1346.

SUBSCRIPTIONS cost $89.00 for individuals and $259.00 for institutions, agencies, and libraries in the United States.

EDITORIAL CORRESPONDENCE should be sent to the Editor-in-Chief, Elizabeth J. Whitt, N473 Lindquist Center, The University of Iowa, Iowa City, IA 52242.

ISBN: 978-1-118-01047-1

www.josseybass.com

CONTENTS

EDITOR'S NOTES

Here, finally, is a publication completely dedicated to strategic planning in student affairs. This volume applies business and nonprofit techniques to higher education, bringing the topic of strategic thinking, planning, and acting to the daily work of the profession. The chapter authors understand the realities of applying strategies from other sectors to higher education—in particular, the work of serving college students in their learning environment. They write from experience and a firm belief that strategic planning, applied appropriately, can mean success for student services in good times and bad.

Some student affairs professionals cringe at the mention of the term *strategic plan*. On one campus I visited, colleagues warned me time and again not to use the phrase since the last implementation of such an effort had resulted in a lot of people losing their jobs. Terminating employees is not the objective of a strategic plan. Others think it is a lot of show without results. The plan sits on a bookshelf in a thick binder, gathering dust. Many say they are engaged in strategic planning, but it is merely operational planning. The inspirational benefits of creating one's own future and aspiring to achieve motivating results are lost on them. One of my staff thinks it is all just the latest trend and a waste of time. Such a person keeps you true to your belief that strategic planning need not be cumbersome, wordy, boring, or the gateway to unemployment. If done right, it is visionary in its goals and exciting in its mandates, and it creates a workplace where the best in the profession seek to be employed and where the students you desire come to learn.

Strategic planning can make the difference on whether student affairs flourishes, survives, or ceases to exist in the rapidly shifting sands of postsecondary education. A well-developed and well-executed strategic plan provides student affairs professionals with the best position to bring visibility and focus to current and future issues. Student affairs professionals who think and act strategically will lead their institution into the future with foresight, flexibility, and purpose.

The profession's historic documents chronicle the ability of student affairs to refocus and achieve outcomes with changes in context and action. This begins with the 1937 *Student Personnel Point of View* by the American Council of Education, which creates "a new type of educational officer" to give faculty more time to teach the preservation, transmission, and enrichment of the important elements of culture. The 1949 *Student Personnel Point of View* reflects the shift to a post–World War II college atmosphere, flooded with worldly GIs, with an emphasis on preserving freedom, responsibilities at home, and democratic principles. The 1994 *Student Learning*

NEW DIRECTIONS FOR STUDENT SERVICES, no. 132, Winter 2010 © Wiley Periodicals, Inc.
Published online in Wiley Online Library (wileyonlinelibrary.com) • DOI: 10.1002/ss.370

Imperative by the Association of College Personnel Administrators acknowledges the throes of transformation that higher education found itself in with global competition, eroding public confidence, accountability demands, and demographic shifts. In 2004 the Association of College Personnel Administrators and National Association of Student Personnel Administrators' *Learning Reconsidered* focused on the campuswide student experience in its argument for the integrated use of all education's resources in the education and preparation of the whole student.

The past illustrates the benefits of forward thinking and planning, as well as the setbacks of avoiding such a challenge due to the daily demands of student services work. The development and implementation of a plan that is strategic about the future will not only ensure survival but will create opportunities for student affairs leadership to thrive on campus. As stated in *Learning Reconsidered* (2004), "A remarkable number of social and cultural trends, economic forces, population changes, new and emerging technologies, and issues of public policy will have powerful and lasting effects on the ability of colleges and universities to fulfill the demands of their mission and the expectations of their students and constituencies" (p. 6). In Chapter One of this volume, I lay out the nuts and bolts of a process to consider these conditions while crafting an effective plan that is a strategic creation of the preferred future for our work and for our constituents.

A strategic plan begins with a student affairs professional's courage to lead change. Leaders do not wait; rather, they shape their own future, which is what strategic planning is all about. This call to action does not preclude the importance of planning to change. In Chapter Two, Kemal Atkins lays out the building blocks for a critical foundation to the work of writing and executing a plan that has buy-in, influence, and transformational outcomes.

The process of creating and carrying out a strategic plan inspires and motivates with a vision that is produced by conviction and ignited by a purpose. Thus, it is a significantly values-laden process for the values-based profession of student affairs. This is critical to the initial steps of the strategic planning process, which Les Cook elaborates on in Chapter Three.

The key component to planning, writing, implementing, and constantly updating a well-done strategic plan is assessment. From beginning to end, data and their analysis are a key driver in setting accurate context for current and future work. Marilee Bresciani drives home the point in Chapter Four that assessment is part of the never-ending cycle of thinking and acting strategically about the work of student services in higher education. The need to revise a course of action or stay with the plan is embedded in the ongoing measurement of impact and achievement of intended outcomes.

Nowhere has this point been driven home more than in the drastic budget reductions forced on student affairs units and their institutions in light of the global economic downturn. The strategic plan has proven itself a valuable partner in the budget allocation and reallocation process and, now, budget-cutting decisions. Jim Conneely writes about the link between strategic planning and financial management in good times and bad in Chapter Five.

A sound monograph on strategic planning in student affairs should include the academic faculty perspective on our work in the collegiate learning environment. In Chapter Six, Rich Whitney provides an original perspective on the work of our profession in setting a course for the future. His academic career was preceded by work in the private sector, then student affairs, and now firmly entrenched in the world of teaching and research. The insight and advice he provides will shape how we successfully include faculty as we create and put forth strategic plans on each of our campuses.

The required flexibility and nimbleness of a strategic plan may have been even more apparent at Tulane University after the devastation caused by Hurricane Katrina. In Chapter Seven, Cynthia Cherrey and Evette Castillo Clark share the realities of a charted course gone awry and the rebuilding of a vision for renewal in the face of long-term diminished resources—mental, physical, and fiscal. If we think strategic planning and implementation are a challenge under normal circumstances, imagine the strategies that must be implemented when the things we take for granted are gone. Planning from long distance without infrastructure and diminished staff and students strewn nationwide requires passion, commitment, and strategic good sense. Tulane's lessons are applicable to us all.

Chapter Eight provides additional proof that a strategic vision can be inspiring, measurable, and achievable. The example of a 2002 strategic plan from the University of Nevada, Reno does more than show how a plan might be presented. It demonstrates the power of articulating organizational values and setting visionary goals for an entire division of student affairs. The achievement of seven themes as varied as enrollment growth, building a new student union, and creating a climate of assessment are the best proof that strategic planning can work.

If the term *strategic plan* conjures up too many negatives for you and your staff, call it a renewal plan, as Tulane did, or a blueprint to the future, or Vision 2020. Whatever works for you will ensure the buy-in necessary to move ahead with achievements you and your colleagues once believed were impossible.

Shannon E. Ellis
Editor

References

American Council on Education. *The Student Personnel Point of View.* Washington, D.C.: American Council on Education, 1937.

NEW DIRECTIONS FOR STUDENT SERVICES • DOI: 10.1002/ss

American Council on Education. *The Student Personnel Point of View.* Washington, D.C.: American Council on Education, 1949.

Association of College Personnel Administrators. *The Student Learning Imperative.* Washington, D.C.: Association of College Personnel Administrators, 1994.

Keeling, R. (ed.) (2004) *Learning Reconsidered.* Washington, D.C.: Association of College Personnel Administrators and National Association of Student Personnel Administrators, p. 6.

SHANNON E. ELLIS is vice president of student services and adjunct faculty in the College of Education at the University of Nevada, Reno.

NEW DIRECTIONS FOR STUDENT SERVICES • DOI: 10.1002/ss

1

This chapter introduces the topic of strategic planning in student affairs by exploring its meaning and relevance to sound management and a force for change. A model is presented for the student affairs strategic planning process and elements of a written plan, including implementation steps.

Introduction to Strategic Planning in Student Affairs: A Model for Process and Elements of a Plan

Shannon E. Ellis

Planning from a strategic perspective has been a mainstay of organizational management for decades. Founded in the private sector, strategic planning is now embraced by the nonprofit world as a catalyst for sound resource allocation, transformative decision making, and motivating staff (Bryson, 1995). It is particularly appealing to higher education in an era of reform caused by public outcry for accountability and affordability. Student affairs professionals who think, plan, and act strategically will ensure maximum benefit to their students and their institution.

On every campus, the role of student affairs increasingly is to bring visibility and focus to current issues and future implications. Strategic planning publicly acknowledges such forces. This chapter applies the literature regarding strategic planning—its meaning, benefits, process, and elements of an effective plan—to the work of student affairs professionals in higher education.

What It Means to Be Strategic

Intentional, futuristic, opportunity seeking, and *nimble* are all words used to describe what occurs when a thought, a plan, or a decision is accurately labeled as being strategic. Add *imagination, cunning, exploration,* and *information analysis* to the definition, and it becomes clear that being strategic

NEW DIRECTIONS FOR STUDENT SERVICES, no. 132, Winter 2010 © Wiley Periodicals, Inc.
Published online in Wiley Online Library (wileyonlinelibrary.com) • DOI: 10.1002/ss.371

holds the potential for new insights and actions that lead to optimal results. Desired change and directed transformation can become the new norm (Bryson, 1995).

If it is true, as Mary O'Hara-Devereaux (2004) claims, that over the past decade, the art of strategy got lost, it is time to bring it back. "Strategy tragedy," she writes, "strikes when leadership digs foxholes to defend against turbulent change and fails to act urgently and radically to ensure the organization's future success" (p. 180). By engaging in strategic thinking, planning, management, and decision making, a student affairs professional can identify and consider a wide array of options through an inclusive process that explores the environment and sets an agreed-on course of action based on *strategy*. In *Strategic Change in Colleges and Universities* (Rowley, Lujan, and Dolence, 1997), strategy is an agreed-on course of action and direction that changes relationships or maintains alignment. In the work of student affairs, this would lead to a better relationship between administrative units that serve students and the larger institutional environment.

Henry Mintzberg's intensive study (1994) on strategic planning found "strategy making to be a complex, interactive, and evolutionary process, best described as one of adaptive learning. Strategic change was found to be uneven and unpredictable . . . especially when the organization faced unpredictable shifts in the environment" (p. 110). O'Hara-Devereaux (2004) describes that environment as "the Badlands, a rugged stretch that bridges the past with the future, a time after massive structural shifts have rendered the old economy and its social foundations obsolete, and new values and structures are not yet firmly in place"(p. 4).

The environment is the political, social, economic, technological, and educational ecosystem, both internal and external, to the higher education institution in which student affairs organizations reside. Strategic planning is the formal process designed to help administrative units identify and maintain an optimal alignment with the most important elements in its environment. From this plan come decisions that best fit the needs of the student affairs and management practices that ensure attention is focused to maintain optimal alignment with the most important elements in the environment (Rowley, Lujan, and Dolence, 1997).

A Word of Caution: Strategic Planning Is Not the Same as Planning. The work of student affairs practitioners often means developing a series of activities aimed at achieving a goal, carrying out a plan, assessing the results, and, based on this, revising, ending, or continuing to implement these initiatives. This can be productive and satisfying work, but it is not strategic.

Mintzberg (1994) states, "This confusion lies at the heart of the issue: the most successful strategies are visions, not plans" (p. 107). Mintzberg describes planning as a "calculating style," while being strategic invokes a "committing style": "Those with a calculating style fix on a destination and calculate what the group must do to get there, with no concern for the members' preferences. But calculated strategies have no value in and of themselves. . . . Strategies take on value only as committed people infuse them with energy" (p. 109).

Strategic planning focuses on a "committing style" that motivates people with high aspirations toward a common vision (Kouzes and Posner, 1995). The challenge and role of a student affairs leader is to create a shared view of what is important, of what matters: "It's a process that detaches strategy from operations, thinking from doing" (Kouzes and Posner, 1995, p. 244). When students affairs is engaged in both thinking and doing, planning and execution become strategic.

What Strategic Planning in Student Affairs Is. Strategic planning is the process of determining what a student affairs organization intends to be in the future and how it will get there. It is finding the best future for the student affairs organization and the best path to reach that destination. Such planning involves fundamental choices about the future of the student affairs unit. These choices include deciding on the mission and what goals to pursue, as well as the programs and services to offer to accomplish this mission. The answers determine how student affairs staff will find and use the resources needed to meet the goals.

The development and management of a strategic plan has been compared to gently steering a ship by changing course a few degrees at a time in response to internal (fuel) and external (weather) elements (Rowley, Lujan, and Dolence, 1997). Saunie Taylor, vice president of student affairs emerita at the University of Arizona, describes it as "changing a tire while the car is moving." What it most definitely is, is a chance to write the future of the student affairs story on one's own campus. As Sam Keen (1989) put forth, "Whoever authors your story authorizes your action" (p. xiv).

A comprehensive strategic plan is crafted to direct student affairs to realize its aspirations more nearly and provide an opportunity to evaluate what it is doing, why it does so, who does it, and how well and how efficiently it is being done. Furthermore, a plan will help determine if the student affairs unit is fulfilling its stated mission (Ern, 1993).

For student affairs practitioners, "strategic planning is charting a course that you believe is wise, then adjusting that course as you gain more information and expertise. A clear sense of mission and direction will guide your choices about which opportunities to pursue and which to avoid" (Barry, 1986, p. 11). The central objective of strategic planning is to position student services so that it can shape and exploit its environment.

Benefits of Strategic Planning to Student Affairs

Student affairs practitioners need to engage in strategic planning for five important reasons.

First, the development and implementation of a strategic plan by student affairs is steeped in research on the needs of current and future students and on an assessment of the effectiveness of people, programs, and services in meeting them. Determining the priorities and allocation of time, money, and expertise with regard to students will rest in the hands of those who know it best and are well prepared to bring about the desired outcomes.

Second, if developing a strategic plan is essential to the future of a college or university (Rowley, Lujan, and Dolence, 1997), then it is vital to creating the effective student affairs division of tomorrow (Askew and Ellis, 2005). The root of such importance is the fact that key areas of institutional enrollment such as recruitment and retention are the responsibility of student affairs. Adequate numbers and appropriate characteristics of students admitted and effective retention initiatives have an impact on everything from funding levels and faculty workloads to the nature of academic programs and student support services.

Third, the goal of strategic planning in student affairs is to agree on a plan by which the organization can establish a position that gives it a unique place within the higher education institution. This can be increasingly difficult given that the mission of nearly all colleges and universities in higher education is to help students learn. The niche for student affairs is increasingly duplicated across campus with special recruitment efforts in academic programs, embedding internships and service-learning in courses, and the establishment of major-specific career centers in academic colleges. Creating a plan that ensures student affairs is adding significant value and moving to the center from the margins is the difference between thriving or becoming extinct.

Fourth, a well-done strategic plan can be a change driver for transformational student affairs leaders and their staff. The process engages everyone in gathering data, having honest conversations with stakeholders as well as one another, dreaming, creating, strategizing, and implementing. After those steps, nothing could remain the same. Even having to change direction, slow down time lines, and reallocate resources as the result of unexpected circumstances like budget cuts and leadership changes cannot stop the force for change that a strategic plan becomes for student affairs. It clearly sets out the priorities and values of the student affairs organization to be used, most of all, when things do not go as planned.

Fifth, an effective strategic planning process and its implementation create a collegial setting for all student affairs professionals. Individuals from diverse components of a student affairs organization work together to describe the current landscape, gather data, meet with stakeholders, and craft the ideal and preferred future for their work with students. The opportunity to have meaningful and strategic conversations around common values, vision, and mission always results in a more unified student affairs organization with inspired and inspiring professionals.

A New View of the Environment with Strategic Thinking

In *Strategic Thinking and the New Science* (1998), T. Irene Sanders writes that the much-needed skill of strategic thinking is the way to anticipate, respond to, and influence change in the environment as it is emerging and before a crisis arises. According to Sanders, "Strategic thinking has *insight* about the present and *foresight* about the future. And the key to both is understanding the *dynamics* of the 'big picture' context in which your decisions are made" (p. 78). Student affairs practitioners can take a "creative look at their future" (O'Hara-Devereaux, 2004, p. 11) by engaging in strategic thinking. Strategic planning is not a substitute for strategic thinking and acting. Bryson (1995) warns, "When used thoughtlessly, strategic planning can actually drive out precisely the kind of strategic thought and action it is supposed to promote" (p. 9).

For student affairs professionals, strategic thinking must be the first step to any strategy development or planning. It begins with an exploration of the environment, which Sanders (1998) describes as "an intuitive, visual, creative process that results in a synthesis of emerging themes, issues, patterns, connections, and opportunities" (p. 162). She suggests "'visual thinking' as the ability to create and interact with images in one's mind" (p. 87)—for example:

- Writing about the current campus environment for student affairs
- Describing it from a student's perspective as well as that of a student affairs practitioner
- Drawing a picture of the current campus context for student affairs work
- Creating a metaphor for the setting in which student affairs exists

Employing such techniques opens the mind to seeing true realities and discovering future possibilities.

Elements of a Strategic Plan

There is no one way to organize a strategic plan. Several templates exist, such as those created for accreditation purposes, business models, and the public sector. A number of those who have written about strategic planning believe mission and vision statements are key to a successful plan (Bryson, 1995; Covey, 2004; Collins, 2001; Rowley, Lujan, and Dolence, 1997), while others struggle with how and when such statements should enter the strategic planning process (Rowley, Thompson, and Strickland, 1996; Matthes, 1993; Byars, 1991). Nonetheless, some basic elements play key roles in moving strategic thinking along into the development of a successful strategic plan (Rowley, Thompson, and Strickland, 1996; Matthes, 1993; Byars, 1991):

NEW DIRECTIONS FOR STUDENT SERVICES • DOI: 10.1002/ss

- A vision statement (what this student affairs organization aspires to be)
- A mission statement (why the student affairs organization currently exists)
- Identification of five- to seven-core organizational values
- A presentation of the student affairs organization's strengths, weaknesses, opportunities, and threats (SWOTs)
- A statement of five- to seven-key goals based on the SWOTs accompanied by key performance indicators (KPIs) to measure their accomplishment
- A resulting action plan to achieve the goals
- Evaluation and assessment of progress in fulfilling the plan

The Strategic Process: The Key to Success

The process of developing a plan for the future that is grounded in context and futuristic in possibilities is not about predicting the future. No student affairs professionals could have predicted the drastic economic downturn, escalating violence on college campuses, and inflationary double-digit tuition increases. The strategic planning process is about sweeping the environment for all possibilities and executing a plan that is flexible, nimble, and responsive to whatever events occur and conditions arise.

Strategic planning for student affairs answers three fundamental questions:

- Where is the student affairs organization now?
- Where do we want the student affairs organization to be in the future?
- How do we plan to get there?

A strategic mind-set that focuses on skill and capability building (Peters, 1987) is needed to answer these questions. This emphasis on adding value to the educational setting through training to prepare to respond with increased flexibility and quality consciousness will sustain a strategic plan through its incarnations and implementation. It is the development and readiness of these skills that allows every member of the student affairs organization to seek out and exploit opportunities rather than focus on static approaches to organizational development.

Elements of a Strategic Planning Process

Many believe that sound strategic direction has never been more important than it is now, which is why the strategic planning process is what matters most (Sanders, 1998; Rowley, Lujan, and Dolence, 1997; Bryson, 1995). The process of developing the strategic plan is close to 100 percent of its value. According to management guru Tom Peters (1987), a good strategic planning process (1) gets everyone involved; (2) is not constrained by overall organizational assumptions; (3) is perpetually fresh, forcing the asking of new questions; (4) is not to be left to planners; and (5) requires lots of "noodling" time and vigorous debate (p. 510).

This bottom-up process fits the diffuse culture of student affairs and most colleges and universities where governance is decentralized (Rowley, Lujan, and Dolence, 1997). It should begin with those who serve students in a variety of face-to-face ways, with students quickly to the mix and at every stage of the process. As the process moves forward, it should seek ideas from student affairs staff in all job titles and salary categories. The process should never lose sight of students and the front line, where the implementation of the plan takes place and has the greatest chance of impact—with success and with failure.

The process should never be the exclusive responsibility of a small group of stakeholders. If the planning and implementation process is to succeed, it must incorporate the views of all the constituencies that will be affected and will have a role in its implementation. Student affairs units are strongly encouraged to create a planning committee that is expansive in its consultation and transparent in its process of analysis and forming recommendations. It should draw in the most respected members of the institution who are known for their knowledge, fairness, and expertise. Planning members do not adopt and implement key steps, but they bring skill and judgment to the process.

Prepare a Context. The history of student affairs reminds us that our work must be considered within the context of issues that influence higher education and its missions (American Council on Education, 1937, 1949; ACPA/NASPA, 1997). Reflecting on the programs and services the student affairs profession has provided to students in the 1950s as compared to the 1970s and now in the twenty-first century, this point is proven time and again. Some of this change has been accomplished through the reactions of student services to such events as the free speech movement of the 1960s and the Americans with Disabilities Act in the 1970s. Other professional transformation has been through the work of reformers such as Bloland, Stamatakos, and Rogers (1994), as well as such futurists as Howe and Strauss (2000) and calls for transformative education such as in Learning Reconsidered 1 (Keeling, 2004) and Learning Reconsidered 2 (Keeling, 2006).

Student affairs does not operate in a vacuum. Social, political, and economic influences continually change and are important to the nature of student affairs work. It is essential that a strategic plan reflect the current and future environment of the student affairs profession. This demands constant reevaluation and reshaping of programs and services. A place to begin is to document the understanding of the higher education landscape held by members of the student affairs organization through research and conversation. By attending conferences, keeping up with the literature, and listening to experts in the field, student affairs professionals will be able to

NEW DIRECTIONS FOR STUDENT SERVICES • DOI: 10.1002/ss

describe the setting in which their institution exists. It then becomes important to use the same resources for gathering knowledge to understand how the student affairs operation fits into the landscape. It is beneficial to articulate the global, national, regional, and local context for the student affairs profession and the specific work in which student affairs practitioners are engaged.

Establishing current context also demands that members of student affairs on campus spend time thinking about the future context. Funding source projections, birth rates, cultural demographics, and workforce development characteristics are examples of existing indicators that should be considered in analyzing the future for the institution and its student affairs division. This analysis becomes the foundation for thinking and acting strategically.

Develop or Clarify the Student Affairs Mission and Core Values. Why does your student affairs division, department, program, or student service exist? What are your student affairs unit's unshakable beliefs that form the foundation of the work you do in student affairs? A mission statement should set out a clear and concise statement that answers that question. It should start with, "We exist to . . . " and conclude with, "We accomplish this by . . . " It may well change over time as the landscape shifts and context evolves. The ongoing process of developing, implementing, and assessing a student affairs strategic plan forces a constant review and updating of the work the unit does with college students. The mission statement must identify the core values that guide the work. Core values, the principles on which all student affairs organizations are built, guide planning, daily operations, programs, and services (Blanchard, 1996). A values statement answers the question, "What do we believe in?" These enduring tenets do not require external justification. They make statements about what is important to your student affairs unit.

Identify Key Stakeholders, and Conduct a Situational Analysis. The effective strategic plan includes an honest assessment of the capabilities, strengths, weaknesses, and limitations of your student affairs operation. Also known as an environmental scan, this is a snapshot of student affairs now and results in an outline of the factors that have an impact on your ability to achieve success. At its best, the evaluation should pertain to the global, national, regional, and local concerns first acknowledged in setting the context for this work. Information and evaluation must be gathered from multiple sources: deans, community members, faculty, staff, donors, parents, and current and prospective students. This valuable and time-consuming step in the process does more than identify strengths, weaknesses, opportunities, and threats. It can dramatically improve relationships. The best review assesses staff, programs, and communications by student affairs units. All stakeholders should have a voice in the planning effort.

NEW DIRECTIONS FOR STUDENT SERVICES • DOI: 10.1002/ss

Clarify the Vision. Clarifying the vision helps every student affairs practitioner remember where the organization is headed. What is the desired future state? It should answer the question, "Where do we want to be?" What does your division aspire to become? A vision is the aspirational statement for a student affairs program. It is the stretch goal that serves to inspire staff toward improved excellence and greater effectiveness in meeting the mission through service to students, faculty, and staff.

Establish Key Performance Indicators. A key performance indicator (KPI) is a measure of an essential outcome of a particular organizational performance activity or an important indicator of the health of the division (Rowley, Lujan, and Dolence, 1997). Be courageous and realistic in setting KPIs. They must be focused on the desired outcomes so that efforts are directed to the right objectives without distraction. KPIs keep student affairs strategic decision making on course. Indicators help all participating decision makers fully explore and understand relationships among the student affairs organization, the desired objectives, and the general environmental forces with which student affairs must deal. The most effective way to do this is to check performance against expectations and those of constituents and stakeholders. The strategic planner is seeking a beneficial link between student affairs and the environments in which the profession must thrive. Examples of KPIs for student affairs work are first-year retention rates, graduation rates, student satisfaction, at-risk student persistence and graduation rates, financial aid distribution, and staff-to-student ratio.

Establish Goals and Milestones. KPIs become broader goal statements with specific objectives. Goals express the aspirations of the student affairs unit, such as an unrelenting pursuit of student satisfaction. Objectives related to the goal are specific targets to be accomplished in a specific time, for example, increasing freshmen retention from 70 to 75 percent in five years. Goals and objectives express desired outcomes for student affairs work and answer the question, "What do we want to accomplish?" Progress should be measurable. Using all the information developed from the previous steps, identify three things for each key performance indicator: (1) the current status, (2) the future goal, and (3) a midpoint milestone (Rowley, Lujan, and Dolence, 1997). A workable strategic plan analyzes the objectives and determines which take precedence. But setting priorities is just the beginning, of course.

Develop Strategies and Implement Action Plans. Strategies are simply the means or general action to be taken to achieve long-term objectives. Action plans are developed by smaller groups such as cross-divisional work teams or a unit within student affairs such as career development. Action plans can be divided into action steps with an individual assigned specific responsibility for achieving a task. An implementation plan identifies in priority order the time lines, budgets, communication flow, and operational tactics necessary to achieve the objectives (Bryson, 1995). It requires a logical procedure with workable strategies to achieve the goals.

Several innovative means exist to carry out a plan. These include focusing on three to five themes that give direction and focus resources. When the themes emerge from the planning process, they will be genuine and have staying power no matter the budget cuts or personnel changes. Themes that emerge tend to mobilize people as they are open to interpretation and discovery. Strategic implementation teams should be developed around each theme where plans evolve to pursue the goals.

Another implementation strategy is to launch a campaign where the focus is on action more than planning. In a campaign, people "act their way into new thinking." Campaigns work particularly well in colleges and universities where authority is diffuse and there are windows of change with budget shifts, leadership turnover, and new academic years. Representational committees are replaced by groups comprising people with passion and interest who move forward with energetic actions that produce pilot programs, experimental probes, and new projects.

A third implementation method links accomplishment of strategic goals to department action plans, resource allocation, and individual performance review ratings. This creates the opportunity for reorganization to achieve the goals, including personnel changes, job description revisions, and program elimination, before additions are made.

Evaluate and Apply Results to the Ongoing Plan. Initially it is important to validate accomplishments honestly. Take time to feel good about successes, and allow yourself to adjust any goals or strategies based on lessons learned. It may even be important to abandon an objective or an action plan and start over. Often a goal or plan is added at some stage in the process. Unexpected developments such as personnel changes and budget adjustments are not uncommon. Hurricanes and pandemics may be rarer but nonetheless cause for flexibility and change. And with changes come calls for reallocation of resources, including time, expertise, and funding within the larger context of the overall strategic plan. At a minimum, this is a stage in the plan and process that calls for revision.

The Finished Document. The final document for the strategic plan must be concise, no more than ten pages with an emphasis on the development of strategic skills. It must not be put on the shelf or be long enough to fit in a notebook. It should be viewed as malleable and living, so that it is used as revised on a daily basis. In other words, it must be a living document, not an icon (Peters, 1987). The content and format of the plan and the process followed to arrive at it should be changed significantly every year. This keeps it from becoming predictable and stale, an institutionalized piece of the bureaucracy. Such changes allow it to remain thought provoking, vital, and useful as an agent for change in a changing environment.

NEW DIRECTIONS FOR STUDENT SERVICES • DOI: 10.1002/ss

You Know It's a Good Plan When It Gets Put to Good Use

A plan that is used every day will help student affairs professionals initiate change, particularly reorganization that can lead to transformation. It can be used to solve problems and address issues, especially those that have been long standing and tolerated out of frustration and lack of resolution strategies. The student affairs strategic plan can be used to assess the effectiveness of how you spend time and money in serving the institutional mission, motivate others and excite yourself, and turn down offers that do not promote the plan. Use it to plan a budget. Most important of all, use it.

References

ACPA/NASPA. *Principles of Good Practice for Student Affairs.* Washington, D.C.: National Association of Student Personnel Administrators and American College Personnel Association, 1997.

American Council on Education. *The Student Personnel Point of View.* Washington, D.C.: American Council on Education, 1937.

American Council on Education. *The Student Personnel Point of View.* Washington, D.C.: American Council on Education, 1949.

Askew, P., and Ellis, S. "The Power of Strategic Planning." NASPA's *Leadership Exchange,* 2005, 3(1)5–8.

Barry, B. W. *Strategic Planning Workbook for Nonprofit Organizations.* St. Paul, Minn.: Amherst H. Wilder Foundation, 1986.

Blanchard, K. *Managing by Values.* San Francisco: Berrett-Koehler, 1996.

Bloland, P. A., Stamatakos, L. C., and Rogers, R. *Reform in Student Affairs.* Washington, D.C.: ERIC Counseling and Student Services Clearinghouse, 1994.

Bryson, J. M. *Strategic Planning for Public and Nonprofit Organizations.* San Francisco: Jossey-Bass, 1995.

Byars, L. L. *Strategic Management.* (3rd ed.) New York: HarperCollins, 1991.

Collins, J. *Good to Great.* New York: HarperCollins, 2001.

Covey, S. R. *The Eighth Habit.* New York: Free Press, 2004.

Ern, E. H. "Managing Resources Strategically." In M. J. Barr and Associates, *The Handbook of Student Affairs Administration.* San Francisco: Jossey-Bass, 1993.

Howe, N., and Strauss, W. *Millennials Rising: The Next Great Generation.* New York: Vintage Press, 2000.

Keeling, R. P. (ed.).*Learning Reconsidered: A Campus-wide Focus on the Student Experience.* Washington, D.C.: American College Personnel Association and National Association of Student Personnel Administrators, 2004.

Keeling, R. P. (ed.). *Learning Reconsidered 2.* Washington, D.C.: American College Personnel Association, Association of College and University Housing Officers-International, Association of College Unions International, National Association for Campus Activities, National Academic Advising Association, National Association of Student Personnel Administrators, and National Intramural-Recreational Sports Association, 2006.

Keen, S. *Your Mythic Journey.* New York: Putnam, 1989.

Kouzes, J. M., and Posner, B. Z. *The Leadership Challenge.* San Francisco: Jossey-Bass, 1995.

Matthes, K. "Strategic Planning: Define Your Mission." *HR Focus,* 1993, 70, 11–12.

Mintzberg, H. *The Rise and Fall of Strategic Planning.* New York: Free Press, 1994.

O'Hara-Devereaux, M. *Navigating the Badlands.* San Francisco: Jossey-Bass, 2004.

Peters, T. *Thriving on Chaos.* New York: Knopf, 1987.

Rowley, D. J., Lujan, H. D., and Dolence, M. G. *Strategic Change in Colleges and Universities.* San Francisco: Jossey-Bass, 1997.

Rowley, D. J., Thompson, A. A. Jr., and Strickland, A. J. III. *Strategic Management.* (9th ed.) Burr Ridge, Ill.: Irwin, 1996.

Sanders, T. I. *Strategic Thinking and the New Science.* New York: Free Press, 1998.

SHANNON E. ELLIS is vice president of student services and an adjunct faculty member in the College of Education at the University of Nevada, Reno.

NEW DIRECTIONS FOR STUDENT SERVICES • DOI: 10.1002/ss

2

Strategic planning can be a powerful instrument in bringing about lasting change to a student affairs organization. Tools and methods to achieve transformation are discussed.

Strategically Planning to Change

Kemal Atkins

The rate of change today requires that each of us become a frantic learner. Otherwise, change will leave us as forgotten in the past. Learning is worthwhile and meaningful in and of itself. Leaders respond to change by learning something. The eager, frantic learners in life find actual joy in the process of change.

Max DePree (2004)

Over the course of my career in higher education, I have either led or participated in numerous strategic planning efforts. While many were successful, I wish more had brought about more lasting change. Kotter (1996) writes, "Powerful macroeconomic forces may grow even stronger over the next few decades. As a result, more and more organizations will be pushed to reduce costs, improve the quality of products and services, locate new opportunities for growth, and increase productivity" (p. 3). American higher education will not be immune to this reality, so senior student affairs officers must help their organizations "leap into the future, overcome their fears, and expand their leadership capacity" (Kotter, 1996, p. 186). Leadership gurus Tom Peters and Nancy Austin (1985) encourage leaders to create successful organizations. For student affairs, this means benchmarking best practices of other universities or programs and identifying qualities such as concern for students, motivated and competent student affairs professionals, a willingness to innovate, and strong leadership that will transform student affairs.

New Directions for Student Services, no. 132, Winter 2010 © Wiley Periodicals, Inc.
Published online in Wiley Online Library (wileyonlinelibrary.com) • DOI: 10.1002/ss.372

How and Why New Leaders Should and Can Use Strategic Planning

Higher education, like the private sector, is searching for innovative ways to respond to demographic shifts, globalization, greater accountability, and new technologies. New organizational models are needed to meet these challenges. In a rapidly changing world, the development of such models can occur through effective strategic analysis and planning. Student affairs, along with their academic counterparts, must show that they function effectively and contribute to student learning and development. Therefore, it is incumbent on leaders in higher education to improve the effectiveness of their institutions.

The strategic process allows exploration and adoption of practices that correlate with the attainment of improved learning outcomes and student success. Jim Collins (2005) describes an organization's work toward achieving such results as "building a framework of greatness: articulating timeless principles that explain why some become great and others do not" (p. 15). According to Collins, five issues principles form this framework:

1. Defining "Great"—Calibrating Success Without Business Metrics
2. Level 5 Leadership—Getting Things Done Within a Diffuse Power Structure
3. First Who—Getting the Right People on the Bus Within Social Sector Constraints
4. The Hedgehog Concept—Rethinking the Economic Engine Without a Profit Motive
5. Turning the Flywheel—Building Momentum by Building the Brand

Strategic planning is a means to build a framework of greatness through which a student affairs division can define its direction. The plan guides decisions on allocating financial and human resources needed to pursue the strategy for achieving desired outcomes. In this age of accountability and increased scrutiny of higher education (especially public higher education), colleges and universities must plan, implement, and measure outcomes more effectively than in the past to serve students better and satisfy key constituencies.

In fact, student affairs practitioners must go beyond traditional strategic planning methods and strive to transform their division and institution to meet the needs of students in the twenty-first century. Often new leaders are brought to an organization because "change is needed." Yes, many will nod, and say that we must change to keep pace with a rapidly changing world, but often we do not really mean it. Nevertheless, success in the twenty-first century, according to Rosabeth Moss Kanter (2001), "requires evolving to a new way of working, a new way of doing business, a new style of human relationships" (p. 16). In her book, *Evolve! Succeeding in the*

Digital Culture of Tomorrow, Kanter asserts that success in this new culture requires a complete makeover, which means that leaders must rethink the model for how to organize the work of the entire organization.

The Bill and Melinda Gates Foundation is an excellent example of a transformational organization that has built its success on its "belief that all people have value" and its fifteen guiding principles that clearly define the foundation's focus, ethics, limitations, possibilities, and willingness to change. The Gates Foundation funding follows its research and knowledge about an effort that has the likelihood to result in lasting change.

The resurgence of Alverno College epitomizes success resulting from innovation in strategic planning. Alverno, a small, urban, Catholic liberal arts college for women, was struggling to define itself at a time when the value of college in general, and a liberal arts education in particular, was being scrutinized nationally. Sister Joel Read, then president of Alverno, led the college's effort to reimagine its mission and made what now are considered two progressive decisions. First, she reorganized the college's class schedule so that Friday afternoons would be set aside for campuswide discussion. Second, she encouraged academic departments to investigate the kinds of questions professionals in their field of study were asking and to determine whether the department's general education curriculum addressed issues related to the field. Alverno responded by implementing a Web-based system that helps students process feedback and take control of their own learning.

Numerous other examples of success achieved through transformational leadership, innovation, and change can be found in business and in higher education. There are even more examples of the organizational failure and mediocrity resulting from their resistance to change. In order for the United States to be more competitive and to prosper, more people need to complete college, and student affairs plays an important role in achieving this goal. Student affairs leaders must start rethinking their organizations and delivery of services. This means planning more strategically to be student centered, strategic in the use of technology, and creative in collaborations with academic affairs and using data to measure success and adjust strategies.

Models and Steps

Student affairs professionals are accustomed to planning for activities, programs, and services that create supportive learning environments on college and university campuses. Strategic planning is different from planning, however, and can often be a painful exercise, primarily because individuals are uncomfortable with change, and strategic planning requires a considerable investment of time. Strategic planning is an organization's process of defining its strategy or direction and making decisions on how its resources will be used to pursue this strategy.

NEW DIRECTIONS FOR STUDENT SERVICES • DOI: 10.1002/ss

Typically a strategic planning initiative is launched when a new leader joins the organization or a plan needs to be updated. Strategic planning has many models from which to choose and includes several steps. There are different names for the steps and the models, and organizations conduct them in a different order. Morley and Eadie's (2001) change portfolio management focuses on identifying concrete initiatives, employed in the short term, that have the promise of achieving significant results. Kotter's (1996) eight-stage change process is a comprehensive planning effort that provides a model for individuals and organizations trying to gain an understanding of change and change leadership. The model provides a road map that can help leaders prepare and implement strategies that make institutions more productive and competitive in this rapidly changing business and academic environment. Before choosing a model or designing a plan, it is imperative to spend time learning the organizational culture. This is particularly important for a new senior student affairs officer. There is no one right way to conduct strategic planning or the change process.

Leaders in student affairs choose to either adopt a particular model that fits or help facilitate the change or transformation they desire. Other student affairs professionals create their own model by selecting best practices from several examples of successful change initiatives. Interviews with senior student affairs officers revealed that this is often the case: they identify the elements of a few models that they determine to be suited for their organization and their leadership style. For example, the division of student affairs at Northern Illinois University (2010) initiated a comprehensive nine-month strategic planning effort to create its plan. The result was an organizational redesign that improved the coordination and delivery of student services, particularly in the area of campus safety and crisis management.

Similarly, the University of North Carolina at Wilmington (2005) has tackled the problem of alcohol and drug abuse by creating innovative substance abuse prevention and education programs. Done well, change initiatives, of which strategic planning is vital, are examples of Peters's (1985) "passion for excellence" that is needed to sustain and improve programs like these.

Tools to Facilitate the Necessary Mentality, Skills, Thinking, Courage, and Time

Change, rather than stability, has become the norm in the business environment, and it is imperative that higher education embrace this reality in order to prepare students. Therefore, student affairs practitioners must gain a pragmatic understanding of the planning process through education and training. A widely used cliché in sports is that success is only 10 percent physical but 90 percent mental. Although the percentages may not be exact, the sentiment seems to be accurate. Student affairs professionals need to be more knowledgeable about and comfortable with the change process.

NEW DIRECTIONS FOR STUDENT SERVICES • DOI: 10.1002/ss

Professional Reading Program. A professional reading program can help student affairs professionals develop a pragmatic understanding of the change process and provide the mental and emotional preparation that will mitigate barriers to change. Many corporations require their supervisors and managers to read certain books, and all branches of the U.S. military have professional reading programs that augment their standard training curriculums. The professional reading program is a systematic way to engage staff in the change process by exploring the literature on planning in depth.

Strategic planning is challenging and requires adequate preparation. Developing a reading program is a low-cost approach to providing professional development opportunities to student affairs personnel. These programs also help to facilitate staff interaction as well as an opportunity for the senior student affairs officer to become more engaged with staff and all levels of the organization.

Typically reading programs involve small groups of employees actively engaged in the material on the selected topic. The approach should be learner centered so that staff will work collaboratively to reflect on and construct meaning for themselves. Furthermore, discussions are at the core of the reading programs. Through these discussions, staff will be able to express their thoughts and feelings about the literature and, more important, gain an understanding of the challenges and practices related to and involved in the change process. The use of technology like e-mail and discussion boards may be introduced to provide staff with resources that go beyond the books and a communication tool for them to continue discussing issues beyond the sessions.

Professional reading programs can help a leader build an internal climate that fosters and celebrates creative thinking and legitimizes the innovation process through serious participation (Morley and Eadie, 2001). Individuals in a student affairs organization need to know that the leader values creativity and welcomes new ideas. Morley and Eadie write that "creativity is essentially the capacity to generate ideas that fuel the innovation process, providing it with the possibilities for change" (p. 17).

This systematic approach to preparing individuals in the organization for planning is a promising strategy to helping staff gain understanding and, with this understanding, inspiration. Ordinary people working together can create extraordinary results in an organization that has an intentional practice that inspires its people. This can be accomplished if the leader is committed to investing the time to gain the commitment of individuals in the organization.

Open Space Technology. A practice known as open space technology is an effective way to identify opportunities for short wins. Open space technology is "a way to enable all kinds of people, in any kind of organization, to create inspired meetings and events" (Herman, 1998, p. 3). Participants in open space meetings, events, and organizations "create and manage their own agenda of parallel working sessions, a central theme of strategic importance" (p. 7).

According to Herman (1998), open space works best when the work to be done is complex, the people and ideas involved are diverse, the passion for resolution (and potential for conflict) is high, and the time to get it done was yesterday. Open space is a simple, powerful way to get people and organizations moving when and where it is needed most. Open space technology can be used to build teams and identify priorities for a student affairs division.

During an open space meeting, participants create a list of challenges and issues for student affairs. The participants rank the items on the lists and divide themselves into groups, based on their interests, to discuss the issues and possible solutions. Throughout the exercise, participants might combine groups to discuss related issues or omit some items altogether. By the end of the meeting, priority issues are identified, teams are formed to develop strategy, and the teams have scheduled their first meeting. In addition, a method of communicating with the entire organization has been determined. Open space technology is an excellent way to take immediate action related to specific issues that the student affairs team has identified as important.

Strategic Change Portfolio Management. Strategic portfolio change management is a systematic approach for producing innovation and concrete results that can be sustained. According to Morley and Eadie (2001), it is a practical method for making a decision about how to invest limited resources beyond the operational plan and budget. This strategic approach is influenced by product research and development work often found in the for-profit world rather than in higher education. Morley and Eadie report that the change portfolio management approach is heavily influenced by the work of Rosabeth Moss Kanter at the Harvard Business School. This approach is recommended as an alternative to the business-as-usual mentality often found within organizations.

The strategic change portfolio management process is guided by a clear strategic framework consisting of values, vision, and mission and process flow through an annual planning stream, parallel to planning and budget preparation. In doing away with the mythical planning hierarchy that has five-year goals and strategies serving as a kind of conceptual umbrella for annual plans, there can be a focus on highest-priority strategic issues. These take the form of opportunities to move toward the envisioned future and of challenges—barriers and threats—that stand in the way of realizing the vision. The result is a generation of strategic change initiatives—practical projects aimed at addressing the selected strategic issues.

Management of these strategic change initiatives occurs in a strategic change portfolio that is kept separate—and protected—from day-to-day operations. Meticulous attention is given to the implementation of these initiatives through a well-defined structure and process.

NEW DIRECTIONS FOR STUDENT SERVICES • DOI: 10.1002/ss

The strategic change portfolio management approach can be applied to produce innovation for individuals, organizational units, and entire institutions. It is especially useful at an institution where the need for change is great in many areas within a student affairs division and resources are limited, which is often the reality. It is important, particularly for a new leader, to identify which areas can be changed or improved within a short period of time (preferably one year) to commit resources that are not part of the day-to-day operations. Morley and Eadie write (2001) that strategic change initiatives that are in one's change portfolio will be diverse—for example, a demand for a student leadership program, the need to streamline a division's budgeting and purchasing process, and improving a damaged relationship with a critical stakeholder.

Developing a Vision and Strategy

Vision is a central component of great leadership. Vision illustrates the future and includes reasons that people should strive to create that future. A vision lists where the institution sees itself in the future and outlines where it wants to be.

The vision for a student affairs division must be aligned with the institution's overall vision. A good vision clarifies the general direction for change, motivates people to take action in that right direction, and helps coordinate the action of different people in a fast and efficient manner. The creation of a vision typically starts with a statement from the organization's leader and reflects that person's ideas and marketplace needs. A steering committee or leadership team typically reviews an existing vision and modifies it according to the leader's ideas, or the team may decide to write an entirely new vision statement. In addition, larger groups of people may become involved in the review and creation of the organization's vision. The visioning process can be messy and is never completed in one meeting. However, when the process is completed, the vision should be one that is shared and embraced by the team.

Change initiatives take time and can easily be derailed if noticeable improvements do not occur relatively quickly. Therefore, it is important that the team identifies opportunities for short wins that help to prevent the change effort from getting off track. By systemically planning for short-term wins, managers increase the likelihood that visible results are produced that give credibility to the transformation effort. "The job of management is to win in the short term while making sure you're in an even stronger position to win in the future" (Kotter, 1996, p. 125). There must be a good balance of leadership and management in order for a change effort to be successful. In a way, the primary purpose of the first six phases of the transformation process is to build up sufficient momentum to blast through the dysfunctional granite walls found in so many organizations. "When we ignore any of these steps, we put all our efforts at risk" (Kotter, 1996, p. 130).

Roadblocks to Effective Strategic Planning

Student affairs leaders must ask themselves and others a number of questions before, during, and after embarking on a change initiative.

- Is our student affairs organization following its strategic plan?
- Did our planning process bring about lasting change?
- Are the right people leading the process?
- Is our organization prepared to plan?

Far too often, even the best-developed plans fall far short of meeting expectations or simply collect dust on office shelves. Leadership teams may lack the experience, motivation, or credibility needed to accomplish the task, or others in the organization are not prepared to be engaged in the planning process.

In *Leading Change* (1996), Kotter addresses the questions that relate to the needs of organizations and individuals in a rapidly changing business environment. He provides valuable examples leaders make when managing change, as well as an eight-step process that can help student affairs leaders transform their organizations.

Kotter (1996, p. 16) identifies eight errors that cause attempts to transform organizations to fail:

1. Allowing too much complacency
2. Failing to create a sufficiently powerful guiding coalition
3. Underestimating the power of vision
4. Undercommunicating of the vision by a factor of 10 (or 100 or even 1,000)
5. Permitting obstacles to block the new vision
6. Failing to create short-term wins
7. Declaring victory too soon
8. Neglecting to anchor changes firmly in the corporate culture

In addition, "Normal human resistance, the pressure of day-to-day events, scarce resources, inadequate planning process; and incomplete information and changing circumstances" (Morley and Eadie, 2001, p. 3) are significant barriers to leading and managing innovation and change. Of these, Morley and Eadie write, it is vital that leaders do not underestimate the power of human resistance, which is rooted in "fear—of being inadequate to the new demands, of failing and suffering humiliation, of being seen as inept or weak, or, if in a position of authority, of having that power and status diminished" (p. 3).

NEW DIRECTIONS FOR STUDENT SERVICES • DOI: 10.1002/ss

Evidence of such errors exists on several college and university campuses. New leaders may arrive at an organization where the status quo was accepted because of complacency. Because there was no sense of urgency, the prevailing thinking was that change was not needed. In some instances staff and institutional leaders needed to blame someone before certain issues could be addressed. Leaders also experience the residual effects of a lack of communication that typically resulted in distrust and where good plans were not implemented because obstacles were allowed to stop progress. Student affairs leaders must be aware of these errors and devise strategies to overcome these and other barriers to transformational change. Thinking about the models that we adopt for strategic planning with the errors in mind is vital to success as a leader.

Conclusion

Far too often, strategic planning efforts are initiated without fully preparing people both mentally and emotionally for the work they are about to undertake. A model for planning may not be clearly articulated to staff. There may not be a broad understanding of the various phases of the change process, much less strategic planning. Student affairs professionals are urged to think of strategic planning in the broader context of transformation and change. Organizations today need to embrace change. Strategic planning can help organizations have improved competitive standards. The key to a successful transformation lies in the preparation of the leadership.

References

Collins, J. *Good to Great and the Social Sectors*. Boulder, Colo.: HarperCollins, 2005.

DePree, M. *Leadership Is an Art*. New York: Dell, 2004.

Herman, M. "What Is Open Space?" 1998. Retrieved July 2, 2009, from http://www.openspaceworld.org.

Kanter, R. M. *Evolve! Succeeding in the Digital Culture of Tomorrow*. New York: McGraw-Hill, 2001.

Kotter, J. P. *Leading Change*. Boston: Harvard Business School Press, 1996.

Morley, J., and Eadie, D. *Leading Change. The Extraordinary Higher Education Leader.* Washington, D.C.: National Association of College and University Business Officers, 2001. Retrieved June 30, 2009, from http://www.acenet.edu/resources/chairs/docs/Morley_LeadingFMT.pdf

Northern Illinois University. Department Chair Online Resource Center. *Strategic Plan 2011–2015*. 2010. Retrieved Feb. 21, 2010, from http://www.stuaff.niu.edu/stuaff/planning/strategic_planning/strategicPlan_2011_2015_webPDF.pdf.

Peters, T. J., and Austin, N. K. *A Passion for Excellence*. New York: Warner Books, 1985.

University of North Carolina at Wilmington. *Strategic Plan*. 2005. Retrieved Feb. 22, 2010, from http://www.uncw.edu/stuaff/strategic.htm.

KEMAL ATKINS *is the vice chancellor for student affairs at Delaware State University.*

3

This chapter explores the role of student affairs and institutional values in strategic planning. It also looks at the historical roots of the profession and methods for incorporating values into planning.

Values Drive the Plan

Les P. Cook

There is no power for change greater than a community discovering what it cares about.

Meg Wheatley (1992)

Like the students we serve on our campuses who are on their own journey of self-discovery, student affairs is on its own journey of discovering professional values. We have designed ways to train, educate, and impress on students the need for a values-based life of engaged citizenship. We appear to be intentional in our design, but our actions are not always congruent. You might say we do not always practice what we preach.

Values-integrated strategic planning provides the opportunity to clarify our professional values as we envision a future that is exciting and perhaps a bit provocative. This chapter explores the role and importance of values in strategic planning and approaches for their inclusion.

The Only Constant Is Change

Student affairs administrators are well aware that change is rampant in the world at large and on campuses. Economic booms and downturns, natural disasters, challenges to provide a safe and healthy learning environment, and finding ways to accommodate the droves of students seeking to enroll are all significant factors driving this change. In these times of change, it is important that institutions remain true to their institutional

NEW DIRECTIONS FOR STUDENT SERVICES, no. 132, Winter 2010 © Wiley Periodicals, Inc.
Published online in Wiley Online Library (wileyonlinelibrary.com) • DOI: 10.1002/ss.373

and professional values but also be willing to embrace change as a compelling reason to embark on a strategic planning process (Sevier, 2000).

In her book, *Leadership and the New Science* (1992), Meg Wheatley, professor, author, and noted management consultant, discusses the work of Ilya Prigogine. His work demonstrates that as systems become more complex, they reach a point of disequilibrium when structures dissipate their energy and begin to recreate themselves in a new form. Wheatley proposes that disequilibrium is an essential condition for growth in organizations. Similarly, as higher education institutions evolve, they too have become far more complex than perhaps is needed. One could also argue that this complexity provides educators a key opportunity to revisit core foundational values, realign where necessary, and strengthen their position going forward. Reflecting on core values is the foundational starting point, and the strengthening can occur through the development and implementation of a well-defined strategic plan.

Strategic planning can occur at any time for institutions that are experiencing this disequilibrium and those that are not. Most often, there is a distinct driving force behind planning efforts; for example, a new president, organizational restructuring, economic pressures, enrollment demands, or changes in curriculum or institutional direction. These winds of change can be stressful, but harnessed correctly, they can become the energy that fuels the organization toward a purposeful destination. Strategic planning can be viewed as an outcome of increased complexity, but it can also provide for renewed creation and growth such as that described by Wheatley (1992).

An integral piece of any strategic planning process is early clarification of the mission, purpose, and values of the organization. The mission and values advocated by most higher education institutions involve providing for the greater good of society. Institutional mission statements offer the framework for decisions and institutional actions. Blanchard and O'Connor (2003, p. 39) describe this alignment as the "managing by values process." It is a three-phased approach: clarifying mission and values, communicating mission and values, and aligning mission and values through daily application. In student affairs, it is critical that time is spent in the early stages identifying the values, mores, and ways of being within the division.

Returning to Our Roots

The history of student affairs makes clear that it is a values-laden profession. The first statement about the student personnel movement by the American Council on Education was the 1937 *Student Personnel Point of View*. It articulated the basic purposes of higher education, the tasks of developing students to their fullest potential for the betterment of society, and a philosophy that clearly delineates that institutions focus on the whole student—body, mind and spirit (Rhatigan, 2009). *The Student Personnel Point of View* was refined in 1949 with renewed emphasis on preservation, transmission, and enrichment of culture. This declaration provided guidance and direction during the early part of the twentieth century, placed emphasis on what is valued, and is found on many campuses today. Both the 1937 and 1949 *Student Personnel Point of View* editions were reconfirmed on the fiftieth anniversary of the original perspective with the 1987 *Student Personnel Point of View*, which reiterated the importance of student affairs work being grounded in the mission of the institution.

During the 1990s, many institutions adopted Boyer's (1990) principles of community, which characterized the college or university campus as sharing values and vision by being:

- A purposeful community
- An open community
- A just community
- A disciplined community
- A caring community
- A celebratory community

Strategic planning and values identification can provide the conduit through which this collaboration occurs as intentional and strategic thinking among different areas and individuals develops (McDonald, 2002).

The emergence of learning as a core student affairs value surfaced in the American College Personnel Association's *Student Learning Imperative: Implications for Student Affairs* (1996). More recently, the role of student affairs in student learning was highlighted in the Association of American Colleges and Universities' *Greater Expectations: A New Vision for Learning as a Nation Goes to College* (2002) and NASPA and ACPA's publication, *Learning Reconsidered: A Campus-Wide Focus on the Student Experience* (Keeling, 2004).

From the *Student Personnel Point of View*, to Boyer's emphasis on community and the more recent focus on learning, the seeds have been planted and the dynamics essential for student success clearly articulated. As stated in *Envisioning the Future of Student Affairs* (American College Personnel Association and National Association for Student Affairs Administrators Task Force on the Future of Student Affairs, 2010), "We must focus on our missions and the values they embody while rethinking the tools—the assumptions, structures, roles, constituents, and partners—that enable us to live by and manifest our core purposes" (p. 16). These variables are important and must be considered as we reexamine the tenets of our profession, determine what we value, and begin the process of strategic planning.

Defining and Refining Student Affairs Values

The historical evolution of the student affairs profession sets the stage for this discussion focusing on values and their role in strategic plan development in student affairs. Values can be defined as enduring or emotional beliefs that help guide human behavior and assist individuals and groups in decision making. They help individuals and organizations understand why they do what they do, and they assist in legitimizing the actions taken. To explain other individuals and other institutions, it is important to develop an understanding of their values, rituals, and cultures (Rokeach, 1973). Those involved set the tone, and actions should mirror the values set.

A values-driven strategic plan identifies and relies on the organization's vision, mission, and values and guiding principles as a tool to help guide and reinforce the strategic direction of the organization. Sevier (2000) indicates that strategic planning sets out how best to respond to the circumstances of the environment, calls for a systematic and focused process where questions about experience and present occurrences can be asked, sets priorities and makes decisions, and is about building commitment to the future.

Many of the models available to assist in strategic plan development allude to the importance of values in the development of the plan. Goodstein, Nolan, and Pfeiffer (1993) outline a process that begins with planning, incorporates building blocks, and concludes with implementation. Elements of planning, according to Askew and Ellis (2005), include defining the context, clarifying mission and goals, establishing goals, conducting a situational analysis of the current state, articulating a vision, developing strategies and an action plan, and evaluating success. There are obviously different processes and methodologies for developing a plan. What is important is that philosophical values, rituals, and ways of being are identified because they are the building blocks that help define the plan.

It is commonly understood that student affairs is committed to students and their success. Young (2003) concludes that an inventory of values in student affairs typically includes a focus on individuals, their context, and caring. Students are viewed as responsible and unique individuals in a context that includes community, equity, and justice. Interwoven with a theme of caring, they all come together to focus on the development of the whole student.

Student affairs practitioners are generally concerned with what the institution values and how congruent these values are with their own (Clement and Rickard, 1992). Bolman and Deal (2000) suggest that culture and core values are increasingly important and acknowledged as the key ingredients that hold the organization together and infuse it with passion and purpose. Core values provide the foundation on which strong organizations are built, and in times of turbulence, they provide the stability essential for progress.

NEW DIRECTIONS FOR STUDENT SERVICES • DOI: 10.1002/ss

Articulating Values

Strategic plans begin by asking these questions:

- Who are we?
- What do we want to be in the future?
- How are we going to get there?

Clarifying and articulating organizational values is critical to answering these strategic planning questions. New chief student affairs officers, departmental directors, and those serving in some other leadership capacity will want to know what the institution values, and those who have been at the institution for a number of years are going to want to set aside some time to gather all there is to know about the department or division they are leading. With luck, there will be past annual reports, accreditation studies, external reviews, or other historical data that provide some perspective on the role of student affairs at the institution as well as the values endorsed.

Involving Your Team and Others. Our core values, driven by our mission, purpose, and people, help us to make sense of our uncertain, ambiguous world. Embarking on the process of clarifying and articulating values for student affairs professionals may seem unwieldy, but once the initial steps have been taken, this process can be quite energizing for those involved. Preparing for the planning process can be critical to the success of planning efforts. In their book, *Applied Strategic Planning* (2008), Nolan, Goodstein, and Goodstein suggest beginning by ensuring that those participating fully understand the process on which they are about to embark, that efforts have been made to evaluate the readiness of the organization for planning, and the necessary framework for planning is in place. Identifying a key group of individuals—a guiding coalition—early on to reflect on the culture, rituals, and values of the division can be well worth the effort, not only for long-term success but also for solidifying the team in the early stages (Kotter, 1996).

In *The Wizard and the Warrior* (2006), Bolman and Deal refer to this individual as the wizard—someone whose strength comes from having wisdom, insight, and the ability to see the big picture. This, coupled with the understanding of the cultures, values, and beliefs of the organization, helps the wizard to be an effective champion. Putting together a team can be very positive when it is done correctly; however, if adequate time and effort are not committed to this process, it can be quite disruptive.

The discussions the planning team pursues early on should focus on an audit of core values: those enduring beliefs or principles the organization embraces and strives to put into action. Facilitating this activity provides the team an opportunity to answer a number of different questions:

- Who are we?
- What do we value?
- What is our philosophy about students? Parents? Others?
- What needs do we fill?
- What is our role in the academy?
- How do we anticipate our role changing?

Who Are We? The process of values clarification affords those involved an opportunity to share their personal values (those that are important to the individual, such as honesty, dedication, faith, and empathy for others), as well as provide an opportunity for the group to articulate those owned and accepted by members of the organization (Nolan, Goodstein, and Goodstein, 2008). Another way this might be accomplished is through a SWOT (strengths, weaknesses, opportunities, threats) analysis (Sevier, 2000) or by conducting a simple gap analysis, which provides the institution the opportunity to evaluate the difference between its current position and its desired future.

What Do We Value? It has been suggested that high-performing organizations share a set of widely shared conventions, principles, or philosophies that guide them, and this is arguably the case in student affairs. Formal mission statements provide the foundation on which institutions rely; they articulate core values, describe aspirational goals, and delineate desired outcomes. The mission of student affairs at Macalester College in St. Paul, Minnesota, clearly articulates what is done and what is valued: "We are catalysts in the construction of intentional learning environments committed to a challenging, student centered education. We partner with students to make the most of their Macalester experiences by supporting their development of reflective leadership, identity exploration, and responsible citizenship" (Macalester, 2010).

Good practice in student affairs requires a commitment to the institutional mission, as well as support of the divisional core values and plan (Reisser and Roper, 1999). The crafting of a mission statement and strategic plan that articulate consistent core values and strategic principles that every follower and stakeholder recognizes and embraces as central to all decisions and organizational actions is critical to the sustainability and success of any institution (Sample, 2002).

What Is Our Philosophy About Students? Parents? Others? Where values provide direction in making decisions, it is important that consideration is also given to the philosophy that drives student affairs work. Is the student affairs model of practice in place more traditionally centered, or is it innovative? A number of different philosophical perspectives can be used as guidance. Traditional models are focused on out-of-classroom administratively or learning-centered philosophies, whereas the innovative model includes a student-centered model and the academic and collaborative model (Manning and Kinzie, 2009).

What Needs Do We Fill? What needs does student affairs fill? The role of student affairs has evolved from the early deans of men and women to play a more integrated and broader role in the academy. As practitioners, we are focused on students' personal and professional growth and development; appreciation of and respect for uniqueness and individuation; holistic learning; engaged citizenry; and so on. Student affairs professionals wear many hats and must be ready to meet the changing needs of individual students, as well as the demands of their institution. Although needs may vary from campus to campus, the primary focus of student affairs has always been and always will be student success and commitment to the development of the whole person (American College Personnel Association and National Association for Student Affairs Administrators, 1996).

What Is Our Role in the Academy, and How Do We Anticipate Our Role Changing? Student affairs is a relatively youthful profession that continues to evolve. As an evolving profession in an environment of change, it is not uncommon for roles to switch and realignments to occur more frequently than before.

Incorporating Values into Planning. Once values have been articulated and agreed on, it is crucial that they not only drive the plan but are infused into planning efforts. The mission statement, driven by the articulated values, becomes the unifying statement that advocates the future direction of the organization. A first-rate mission statement is clear and understandable, credible, brief, focused, and flexible (Nolan, Goodstein, and Goodstein, 2008). Once the mission and values have been articulated, it is imperative they are communicated and evident in all that is accomplished.

Congruency with Institutional Mission and Vision. It would be difficult to live the values and achieve the mission of the institution if they have not been clearly defined, and it would be even more problematic if the mission of student affairs is not congruent with the institutional mission. Duke University provides an institutional mission that demonstrates congruency. The mission of Duke University (2001)

> is to provide a superior liberal education to undergraduate students, attending not only to their intellectual growth but also to their development as adults committed to high ethical standards and full participation as leaders in their communities; to prepare future members of the learned professions for lives of skilled and ethical service by providing excellent graduate and professional education; to advance the frontiers of knowledge and contribute boldly to the international community of scholarship; to promote an intellectual environment built on a commitment to free and open inquiry.

Congruence is evident in Duke's student affairs mission statement (Duke University, 2009) which "is to support the optimal growth and development of our students and to provide services and support that will enhance their intellectual, social, cultural and physical development."

NEW DIRECTIONS FOR STUDENT SERVICES • DOI: 10.1002/ss

In *Student Success in College: Creating Conditions That Matter* (2005), Kuh and Associates identify six conditions that contribute to the success of students on campus. These are

1. "Living" Mission and "Lived" Educational Philosophy
2. An Unshakeable Focus on Student Learning
3. Environments Adapted for Educational Enrichment
4. Clear Pathways to Student Success
5. An Improvement-Oriented Ethos
6. Shared Responsibility for Educational Quality

These conditions are worthy of consideration and can serve as a guide in student affairs organizations that are in the process of integrating values into strategic planning efforts. In addition to those recommendations are Whitt's (2006) suggestions for student affairs:

- Focus on the educational mission.
- Create and sustain partnerships for learning.
- Hold all students to high expectations for learning and engagement both in and out of the classroom.
- Establish early warning systems.
- Inform students early on what it takes to be successful.
- Recognize the importance of and celebrate diversity.
- Invest resources wisely in programs and people that support student success and learning.
- Create spaces for learning.

These suggestions can provide a baseline for beginning the values discussion or a framework for the plan development.

Beyond the mission statement formulation, numerous other steps, outlined in the following chapters, are essential to strategic planning efforts. The core values in student affairs are focused on the growth and development of students and their success, but they have been expanded in recent years to encompass a broader role in learning.

Gauging Success. Nowhere is the adage that actions speak louder than words more apparent and noticeable than on a college or university campus. Once values have been articulated and the plan solidified, student affairs leaders will want to spend some time assessing progress. The bulk of this chapter has addressed values and their implications for planning. Institutional values drive the mission, the mission drives the plan, and the plan drives behavior. A variety of methods can be used to determine if planning efforts have been successful, and they are discussed in Chapter Four.

The mission of the University of Michigan (2010) is "to serve the people of Michigan and the world through preeminence in creating, communicating, preserving and applying knowledge, art, and academic values and in developing leaders and citizens who will challenge the present and enrich the future." The university is characterized by progressive thought and an ethos of excellence. At California State University, Monterey Bay (2005), the mission is "to build a multicultural learning community founded on academic excellence from which all partners in the educational process emerge prepared to contribute productively, responsibly, and ethically to California and the global community." This mission is clearly reinforced by the values the university embraces: applied, active, and project-based learning activities; interdisciplinary studies; multicultural and global perspectives; technological sophistication; service-learning; ethical reflection and practice; and collaboration.

Another way of gauging success is to consider student affairs branding to weave together all of the pieces that help form institutional identity (Sevier, 2002): ideas and attitudes, personalities, emotions, and characteristics, as well as names, symbols, and experiences (Hatch and Schultz, 2008). Brand is demonstrated by how the organization behaves or what you do and what your stakeholders value. Branding is basically institutional values taking on a narrative form.

At Miami University in Ohio (2010), the mission is "developing Miami students who are critically reflective and engaged contributors to a global society, effective communicators, rigorous scholars, and willing team members who welcome the challenge of work on behalf of their communities." Miami University has embraced its brand by developing programs that support this mission, including intentional opportunities for community service and engagement and leadership opportunities through programs like the Harry T. Wilks Leadership Institute and the Cliff Alexander Office of Fraternity and Sorority Life and Leadership.

Other ways of gauging success are examining the data gathered about students: enrollment trends, retention rates, student satisfaction, engagement of students in learning, and other measures of student success. Part of this equation also includes looking at how student affairs and the institution define student success. For some institutions, this is defined by retention, years to graduation, and placement rates; others may view continuous student enrollment or completion of one course as student success.

As institutions examine the strategic planning process and consider how to measure success, it may be valuable to take a lesson from author Jim Collins. In his most recent book, *How the Mighty Fall* (2009), he articulates reasons that leading organizations have fallen from levels of greatness to merely surviving. Collins suggests that as organizations become more and more successful, they develop an arrogance that causes them to lose sight of how they created their success. Organizations, he explains, tend to exhibit an undisciplined pursuit of more. As red flags and early warning signals show up, leaders tend to minimize the not-so-good news; and once success starts to melt, leaders try to find new strategies, but this effort is usually short-lived.

The most evident lesson from this book is that when organizations fall into decline, those that have survived have refocused on their core values and used these values to recalibrate direction rather than waiting for outside forces to dictate their direction. This important lesson is valuable to student affairs and reconfirms the critical lifesaving nature of values in strategic planning efforts. It could be argued that nowhere else are people more important to the work that must be done than in the field of student affairs. If this is true, then Collins's recommendations might provide a methodology for gauging success a place to begin the discussion of values.

Conclusion

Our values drive the mission, and the mission drives the strategic plan. This is integral to our future and to help us to imagine it. Doing this can be both energizing and uplifting and is perhaps best summarized by Olympic snowboarder Shaun White, who said, "We try to break the boundaries and see what we can do. I think we're just tapping into what is possible. I wish I could predict the future. We have to go create it. It's a cool position to be in" (USA Today, 2010).

In his 2010 State of the Union Address, President Barack Obama stated, "In the end, it's our ideals, our values that built America—values that allowed us to forge a nation made up of immigrants from every corner of the globe; values that drive our citizens still. . . . These aren't Republican values or Democratic values that they're living by; business values or labor values. They're American values"(ABC News, 2010). This too holds true in student affairs. Student affairs professionals in all institutions—community college of four-year university, private or public, liberal arts or research-based institution—are committed to student success. This success always has been and always will be our most important endeavor; these values are the driving force in planning efforts and must be evident throughout our work.

As stated in *The Principles of Good Practice for Student Affairs* (American College Personnel Association and National Association for Student Affairs Administrator, 1996), the choice for student affairs is quite simple: we can pursue a course that immerses us in the central mission of our institutions by working with faculty colleagues and others, or we can retreat to the margins and hope to avoid the inconvenience of change. As student affairs professionals, we value students, their success, and making a difference in their lives. Retreating is not an option.

References

ACPA/NASPA *Principles of Good Practice for Student Affairs*. Washington, D.C.: National Association for Student Affairs Administrators and American College Personnel Association, 1997.

American Association of State Colleges and Universities. *The American Democracy Project*. Washington, D.C.: American Association of State Colleges and Universities, 2003.

American College Personnel Association. *The Student Learning Imperative: Implications for Student Affairs*. Washington, D.C.: American College Personnel Association, 1996.

American College Personnel Association and National Association for Student Affairs Administrators. Task Force on the Future of Student Affairs. *Envisioning the Future of Student Affairs*. Washington, D.C.: American College Personnel Association and National Association for Student Affairs Administrators Task Force on the Future of Student Affairs, 2010.

American Council on Education. *The Student Personnel Point of View*. Washington, D.C.: American Council on Education, 1937, 1939, 1949, 1987.

Askew, P., and Ellis, S. "The Power of Strategic Planning." NASPA's *Leadership Exchange*. 2005, *3(1)* 5–8.

Association of American Colleges & Universities, *Greater Expectations: A New Vision for Learning As a Nation Goes to College*, Washington, D.C. 2002.

Blanchard, K., and O'Connor, M. *Managing by Values*. San Francisco: Berrett-Koehler, 2003.

Bolman, L., and Deal, T. *Escape from Cluelessness*. New York: AMACOM, 2000.

Bolman, L., and Deal, T. *The Wizard and the Warrior: Leading with Passion and Power*. San Francisco: Jossey-Bass, 2006.

Boyer, E. *Campus Life: In Search of Community*. Princeton, N.J.: Carnegie Foundation for the Advancement of Teaching, 1990.

California State University–Monterey Bay. "Mission Statement." 2005. Retrieved February 9, 2010 from http://csumb.edu/site/x11551.xml.

Clement, L., and Rickard, S. *Effective Leadership in Student Services: Voices from the Field*. San Francisco: Jossey-Bass, 1992.

Collins, J. *How the Mighty Fall and Why Some Companies Never Give In*. New York: HarperCollins, 2009.

Duke University. "Mission Statement." 2001. Retrieved February 12, 2010 from http://www.trustees.duke.edu/governing/mission.php.

Duke University. "Student Affairs Mission Statement." 2009. Retrieved February 12, 2010 from http://www.studentaffairs.duke.edu/ovp/mission.

Goodstein, L., Nolan, T., and Pfeiffer, J. *Applied Strategic Planning: How to Develop a Plan That Really Works*. New York: McGraw-Hill, 1993.

Graves, W. (2010, February 18) White's Showstopper Caps Olympic Gold. *USA Today*. Retrieved from http://sports.yahoo.com/olympics/news?slug+txsbdmenshalfpipe.

Hatch, M. J. & Schultz, M. *Taking Brand Initiative: How Companies Can Align Strategy, Culture, & Identity Through Corporate Branding*. San Francisco: Jossey-Bass, 2008.

Keeling, R. P. (ed.). *Learning Reconsidered: A Campus-Wide Focus on the Student Experience*.Washington, D.C.: American College Personnel Association and National Association of Student Personnel Administrators, 2004.

Kotter, J. *Leading Change*. Boston: Harvard Business School Press, 1996.

Kuh, G., and Associates. *Student Success in College: Creating Conditions That Matter*. San Francisco: Jossey-Bass, 2005.

LeaderShape. *LeaderShape Institute Facilitators Manual*. Champaign, Ill.: LeaderShape, 2006.

Manning, K., and Kinzie, J. "How About Changing Your Student Affairs Organization? Some Ideas from the Field." Program session presented at the National Association of Student Personnel Administrators Annual Conference, Seattle, Mar. 2009.

McDonald, W. *Creating Campus Community: In Search of Ernest Boyer's Legacy*. San Francisco: Jossey-Bass, 2002.

Miami University of Ohio. "Student Affairs Vision: Creating Global Citizens, Leaders, and Life-Long Leaders." Retrieved March 1, 2010 from http://www.units.muohio.edu/saf/.

Michigan Technological University. "Student Affairs: Mission and Goals." Retrieved January 28,2010 from http://www.sa.mtu.edu/vp/mission.html.

Nolan, T. Goodstein, L., and Goodstein, J. *Applied Strategic Planning*. San Francisco: Jossey-Bass/Pfeiffer, 2008.

Obama, B. http://abcnews.go.com/Politics/State_of_the_Union/state-of-the-union-2010-president Retrieved January 29, 2010.

Reisser, L., and Roper, L. "Using Resources to Achieve Institutional Missions and Goals." In G. Blimling and E. Whitt (eds.), *Good Practice in Student Affairs: Principles to Foster Student Learning*. San Francisco: Jossey-Bass, 1999.

Rhatigan, J. "From the People Up: A Brief History of Student Affairs Administration." In G. McClellan and J. Stringer (eds.), *The Handbook of Student Affairs Administration*. (3rd ed.) San Francisco: Jossey-Bass, 2009.

Rokeach, M. *The Nature of Human Values*. New York: Free Press, 1973.

Sample, S. *The Contrarian's Guide to Leadership*. San Francisco: Jossey-Bass, 2002.

Sandeen, A. *The Chief Student Affairs Officer*. San Francisco: Jossey-Bass, 1991.

Sevier, R. *Strategic Planning in Higher Education: Theory and Practice*. Washington, D.C.: CASE Books, 2000.

Strange, C., and Banning, J. *Educating by Design: Creating Campus Learning Environments That Work*. San Francisco: Jossey-Bass, 2001.

University of Michigan. "Mission Statement." 2010. Retrieved January 20, 2010 from http://www.umich.edu/pres/mission.php.

Wheatley, M. *Leadership and the New Science: Learning About Organization from an Orderly Universe*. San Francisco: Berrett-Koehler, 1992.

Whitt, E.www.sc.edu/fye/resources/assessment/essays/Kuh-1.19.06.html Retrieved September, 17, 2010.

Young, R. "Philosophies and Values Guiding the Student Affairs Profession." In *Student Services: A Handbook for the Profession*. Komives, S, Woodard, D & Associates (Eds.) San Francisco: Jossey-Bass, 2003.

Les P. Cook is vice president for student affairs at Michigan Technological University.

Adopting the practice of systematically and strategically gathering data to inform the development and implementation of a strategic plan will ensure its achievement. This chapter presents a combination of techniques for student affairs professionals to conduct data-driven planning.

Data-Driven Planning: Using Assessment in Strategic Planning

Marilee J. Bresciani

Data-driven planning or evidence-based decision making represents nothing new in its concept. For years, business leaders have claimed they have implemented planning informed by data that have been strategically and systematically gathered (Banta, Jones, and Black, 2009; Bresciani, 2006; Maki, 2004; Schuh and Associates, 2009; Suskie, 2009; Upcraft and Schuh, 1996). Therefore, it is safe to assume that the concepts that are included in data-driven planning have been around for years. Within higher education and student affairs, there may be less evidence of the actual practice of systematically and strategically gathering data to inform planning.

Data-driven planning is often referred to in higher education as outcomes-based program review. The Western Association of Schools and Colleges (WASC) defines outcomes-based program review as a cyclical process for evaluating and continuously strengthening the quality and currency of programs. The evaluation is conducted through a combination of self-evaluation and peer evaluation by reviewers external to the program or department and, usually, external to the organization (Jenefsky and others, 2009). The results of this process inform strategic planning.

For purposes of this chapter, data-driven planning is defined as a systematic process that gathers programmatic outcomes-based assessment data (for example, data derived from outcomes-based program review) and merges those data with trend, forecast, and capacity data, as well as institutional goals and vision. The results of this process are then used to plan resources, policies, and program design to achieve or refine the intended

NEW DIRECTIONS FOR STUDENT SERVICES, no. 132, Winter 2010 © Wiley Periodicals, Inc.
Published online in Wiley Online Library (wileyonlinelibrary.com) • DOI: 10.1002/ss.374

institutional vision and goals. For student affairs professionals, this means that strategic planning cannot be done in isolation of university data, such as an understanding of market demand for majors, the pool of prospective students, and the institutional learning outcomes and core values. Informed by these data, student affairs professionals must align each portion of their divisional strategic planning with the overall values of the university.

For the profession of student affairs, this means that results derived from outcomes-based assessment processes inform action planning and budgeting. This also means that as the student affairs division staff members gather more data on how well they are meeting institutional priorities, they can also use the same process to demonstrate achievement of their own divisional priorities and goals. Departments within the division can use this process to demonstrate how they are meeting division priorities as well. This chapter provides an overview of the components of and steps to establishing such a process.

Steps for Data-Driven Planning in Student Affairs

When organizations embark on strategic planning, key steps must be put into place. Data-driven planning does not replace those steps; rather, it is intended to contribute to the refinement of those steps by purposefully integrating planning, assessment, and budgeting processes. For example, when an organization decides through strategic planning that it will become the first-choice regional provider of quality education for first-generation students, it begins to design goals that will help it realize that vision. The strategic plan represents the ideal of what the institutional leadership desires to achieve.

Once the strategic plan is put into place, indicators of success are articulated, and programs are often asked to illustrate how they are achieving the goals and indicators represented by the strategic plan (Drucker, 2000; Fullan and Scott, 2009; McClellan, 2009). The challenge here is that key steps, discussed in this chapter, are occasionally left out in implementation. And the result is that organizational members may become frustrated that the organization's vision or strategic plan is not being fully realized. In order to address this initial challenge, it may become important for institutional and divisional leadership to follow some basic steps for data-driven planning. The intent of sharing these suggested steps is to provide institutional and divisional leadership with a framework to consider as they adapt each step, cognizant of their own institutional culture. In many cases, institutions and student affairs divisions already have many of these pieces of data-driven planning in place; they have just not yet pulled them together into a systematic, integrated process.

In order to aid readers with determining how they can pull their processes together to formulate data-driven planning, the proposed steps that follow are intended to be used as guidelines as opposed to procedures that must be followed in the exact order indicated. The steps are not designed as a linear process. You may find, if you follow the steps in numerical order, that when you get to, say, step 4, you may need to go back and refine steps 2 and 3 because you realized that you were collecting data that will not really inform your strategic plan. Or you may choose to engage in step 1 and then step 4 in that order to figure out how to best approach steps 2 and 3. Thus, the steps are to be used as guidelines in any order that makes sense for your division or institution. As usual, institutional and divisional leaders will need to adapt these steps in accordance with their own culture, dynamics, and resources in order to improve their data-driven planning processes (Banta and others, 2009; Bresciani, 2006; Maki, 2004; Schuh and Associates, 2009; Suskie, 2009).

Step One: Establish a Strategic Plan. Many chapters in this book discuss the importance of having a strategic plan and illustrate various ways to accomplish it. The important piece of information to note here is that there must be an institutionally and divisionally agreed-on strategic plan from which to work (Bresciani, Gardner, and Hickmott, 2009; Bresciani, 2006; Schuh and Associates, 2009). Many professionals become frustrated when there is no agreed-on direction for their organization, and thus, the following steps become even more challenging to implement (Drucker, 2000; Fullan and Scott, 2009; McClellan, 2009). In an institution that is not engaged in strategic planning and therefore lacks institutional values and goals with which to align, this process then starts at the division level.

Step Two: Gather Forecast and Trend Data Sometimes the best strategic plans and the most inspiring visions and goals can go unrealized because the planning to create those strategic goals has been done without considering what the forecast or trend data are illustrating. Forecast and trend data simply attempt to calculate or predict some future event or condition. A detailed study or analysis usually informs this type of conversation (Schuh and Associates, 2009).

The types of data used in forecasting and determining trends are typically institutionally reported. They are often collected and stored by agencies outside the institution—for example, extracts from the College Board data sets or other types of national data sets, such as those gleaned from the Common Data Set, the National Clearinghouse, or the Integrated Post Secondary Education Data System. Trend data can also be gleaned from admissions applications, the National Survey of Student Engagement, the Community College Survey of Student Engagement, the Cooperative Institutional Research Program, the College Student Experiences Questionnaire, or Your First College Year surveys. Years of gathering these types of data can illustrate certain trends that can be used in informing whether your strategic initiatives are feasible. (An example is provided later in this section.)

These types of data are often collected or stored at the institutional level. The institutional research office is a good place to start when looking to access and use data that will help in forecasting and identifying trends. If the institutional research office is too busy to assist right away, and it often is, consider contacting the Association for Institutional Research, which has a wealth of resources to assist institutional administrators with this type of institutional data gathering.

In gathering and using data for forecasting or determining trends, the idea is not to become consumed by data but rather to use the data to determine if your strategic goals can be achieved. Perhaps your university vision is to become the first-choice regional provider of quality education for first-generation students. Using this example, your strategic plan has informed a design to implement interventions that will aid first-generation students in their success, but your current plan has no goals to change its outreach processes and plans. In accessing admissions applications data and College Board data, you may discover that the number of first-generation students applying and being accepted by your institution is declining. This would indicate that your vision and your corresponding strategic plan would not be realized unless you also have some initiatives to change outreach to and recruitment of first-generation students.

Before adjusting your strategic plan to focus on a change in outreach and recruitment, you access data from the College Board to identify how many regional students are graduating from high school, taking college placement tests, and being identified as first generation. If you see that the number is high, you can then determine that efforts to develop outreach and recruitment plans may be worthwhile. However, if you discover that the first-generation students graduating from high school are low in numbers and appear to have been decreasing, you may want to reexamine your institutional vision altogether. Institutional and student affairs divisional leadership could also choose to design different types of interventions that work collaboratively with local high schools to increase the number of college-bound first-generation students.

Step Three: Conduct a Capacity Review. Trend data as well as additional types of data, such as financial records, financial forecasting, and capital assets, can also be useful in determining the institution's capacity to meet the strategic plan. Borrowing from the Western Association of Schools and Colleges (2008), a capacity review determines whether an institution has the resources to fulfill its strategic mission. In other words, can the institution function "with clear purposes, high levels of institutional integrity, fiscal stability, and organizational structures and processes to fulfill its purposes?" (p. 30).

Identifying meaningful data that indicate whether an institution or division has key institutional resources, structures, and processes in place to fulfill its institutional or divisional mission and strategic plan is important in determining whether changes need to be made in strategic priorities. Consultation with the institutional research office may enable you to identify, access, and use the most appropriate data to inform your planning.

In order to understand how to use these types of data, we return to our example. Consider that your trend data forecast an increase in first-generation graduates intending to take college entrance exams from your regional high schools, so you know you will have plenty of students applying to your college. However, the data from the College Board also indicate that these students will need more financial aid in order to attend college in the future. Your forecast data show steadily increasing tuition, and your capacity study reveals less available institutional and state grant aid. How do you factor this very real scenario into your strategic planning? What other types of data may you need to collect to make an informed decision?

The idea behind conducting short but informative capacity reviews is that if you are able to identify immediate limitations in the ability to provide the resources needed for realizing the strategic plan, then you may be able to immediately adjust your strategic plan to better reflect your capacity. Or you may choose to adjust the strategic plan to build capacity. The building of capacity to achieve the strategic plan may well become a large portion of that plan.

Step Four: Articulate Indicators of Success. Leaders who are operationalizing their strategic plans may clearly articulate the goals derived from the plan, yet not have clearly identified the indicators of success that directly relate to the goals derived from the strategic plan. Rather than just selecting indicators of success that are easy to measure, consider starting by spending time describing what a successful strategic plan looks like when it is implemented (Banta and others, 2009; Bresciani and others, 2009; Bresciani, 2006; Maki, 2004; Schuh and Associates, 2009; Suskie, 2009).

Indicators of success "are quantifiable measurements, agreed to beforehand, that reflect the critical success factors of an organization. They help an organization define and measure progress toward organizational goals" (Reh, 2009, paras. 1, 2). Such indicators are typically gathered and disseminated at the institutional level, but what types of data should an institution collect in order to be able to provide such indicators of success?

Returning to our example, what would it look like when your institution is the first-choice regional provider of quality education for first-generation students? The initial inclination of planners is to jump to performance indicators that articulate expectations for numbers of admits, persistence, graduation, and career placement rates. These indicators are easy to measure and certainly would make sense to report in relationship to achievement of this vision. But what else do we know about first-generation learners? Would we also want to be able to determine how well the environment welcomes first-generation learners and their families and

New Directions for Student Services • DOI: 10.1002/ss

guardians? How integrated are the services and interventions designed to support these learners (Kuh and Associates, 2005)?

The idea of this step is to indicate purposefully which indicators will be institutionally identified to determine success of the strategic plan (for example, persistence rates, placement rates) and which will be gleaned from more specific programmatic outcomes-based assessment results (for example, evidence of the effectiveness of various and specific student support programs).

Step Five: Prioritize Action Plans to Meet the Strategic Goals. Assuming that your organizational strategic plan has articulated goals or objectives, consider prioritizing them if possible. (Chapter One details steps for goal setting and action planning.) This will assist with prioritizing the action plans that operationalize the strategic plan, which in turn helps prioritize the resources that will enable the strategic plan to come to fruition. When institutional leadership prioritizes the strategic plan goals, faculty and staff are more likely to feel empowered in prioritizing their investment of their own time in their action plans in order to meet the strategic plan (Banta and others, 2009; Bresciani and others, 2009; Bresciani, 2006; Jenefsky and others, 2009; Schuh and Associates, 2009; Suskie, 2009).

In order to prioritize decisions that align with organizational goals, values, and strategic initiatives, criteria must be considered that will assist in the alignment of proposed action plans to the organizational goals, values, and strategic initiatives. Although this chapter cannot anticipate the types of criteria that may best represent various organizational structures, the following questions, adapted from Fred McFarlane (personal communication, February, 12, 2007), former department chair of administration, rehabilitation, and postsecondary education at San Diego State University, may assist institutions in formulating their own criteria:

- How well does the proposed action plan fit with our organizational goals, values, and strategic initiatives?
- Within that fit, how will the action plan benefit current students (for example, residential students, commuters, first generation)?
- How will the proposed action plan affect future students (for example, recruitment, new student populations, and their progression from undergraduate to graduate degrees)?
- How will the proposed action plan increase the impact of the department in relationship to the goals and sustaining objectives of the department and the division?
- How will we know whether the proposed action plan will be effective in increasing the impact of the department on the students?
- Does the proposed plan meet the criteria in that it is consistent with our values and beliefs (for example, access, equity, and student success), financially viable (for example, does it cover the costs, and

can it be leveraged for continued development; note that one-shot efforts take a great deal of time and often diffuse resources and energy), consistent with our professional development, and consistent with our passion and commitment to student learning and development?

Posing such questions begins to develop criteria for prioritizing current outcomes as well as the great ideas for improvements that result from engaging in outcome-based assessment (see step 7).

Step Six: Align Division Resources with Institutional Priorities. This step may appear a bit similar to previous steps, but nevertheless it is important to consider. The prioritization of the division resources toward strategic initiatives influences the availability of resources to improve more refined levels of action plans. And the decisions to refine the actions plans are informed by results of outcomes-based assessment (see step 7). If your institution is bound by a governance structure that gives you very little room to allocate resources in accordance with your strategic plan, then this step will be very quick for the institution to complete, because you are constrained by an inability to prioritize the resources on your own. If the institutional governance allows more flexibility in the allocation of resources, then the idea is to make available certain resources for the improvement and refinement of strategic priorities that can be allocated based on the results of outcomes-based assessment or on the proposals of innovative action plans to improve strategic indicators and initiatives.

Step Seven: Implement Outcomes-Based Assessment Program Review. Implementing outcomes-based assessment plans for the action plans to achieve the strategic plan will help in gathering meaningful data about how well you are achieving your strategic plan. If assessment is done well, the results will yield specific information on what needs to be improved in order to refine the strategic indicators articulated in step 4 (Banta and others, 2009; Bresciani, 2006; Bresciani and others, 2009; Jenefsky and others, 2009; Maki, 2004; Schuh and Associates, 2009; Suskie, 2009).

The following sections set out typical components of an assessment plan and report.

Program Name. The program name helps indicate the scope of the assessment project. Are you planning on assessing a series of workshops within the leadership development center, or on evaluating the entire leadership development center? Often it is difficult to determine the scope of an assessment plan (Schuh and Associates, 2009). When in doubt, organize the plan around programs that have autonomous outcomes (Bresciani and others, 2004; Bresciani and others, 2009).

Program Mission or Purpose. List the program mission or purpose statement. It may also be helpful to provide a one- or two-sentence explanation of how this program mission or purpose aligns with the department, college, division, or university's mission within which it is organized. Setting this out will help explain how the program aligns with institutional values and priorities.

Program Goals. Goals are broad, general statements of what the program wants students to be able to do and to know or what the program will do to ensure what students will be able to do and to know. Goals are not directly measurable. Rather, they are evaluated directly or indirectly by measuring specific outcomes derived from the goals (Bresciani and others, 2004; Bresciani and others, 2009). The further alignment of each goal to department, college or division, or university goals or strategic initiatives generated from the strategic plan assists with the communication of priorities and allows programs to show how they are operating within stated priorities. In addition, the alignment of each goal with professional accreditation standards, if applicable, allows you to determine how this program intends to meet higher-level organization goals and strategic planning initiatives.

Outcomes. Outcomes are more detailed and specific statements derived from the goals. They specifically are about what you want the end result of your efforts to be. In other words, what do you expect the student to know and do as a result of, for example, a one-hour workshop, one-hour individual meeting, Web site instructions, or series of workshops? Outcomes do not describe what you are going to do to the student, but rather how you want the student to demonstrate what he or she knows or can do (Bresciani and others, 2004; Bresciani and others, 2009).

In addition, you want to be able to align each outcome with a program goal. This alignment allows you to link your outcomes to department, college or division, or university goals and strategic initiatives, as well as professional accreditation standards. Such alignment allows you to determine how this program intends to meet higher-level organization goals and strategic planning initiatives.

Planning for Delivery of Outcomes. This is where action planning comes into the process. Here is where you describe or simply draw a diagram that explains how you plan for the student to learn what you expect the student to learn in order for the outcome to be met. Do you plan for the students to learn what you expect them to in a workshop, one-on-one consultation, or a Web site? Simply indicate all the ways in which you provide students the opportunity to achieve the learning outcome. Identifying where outcomes are being taught or delivered also provides reviewers with opportunities to identify where that outcome may be evaluated.

Evaluation Methods and Tools. Often the evaluation method or tool section of the assessment plan can be intimidating to practitioners. This section is not intended to include detailed research methodology. It is intended to simply describe the tools and methods (for example, observation with a criteria checklist, survey with specific questions identified, essay with a rubric, role-playing with a criteria checklist) you will use to evaluate the outcomes of participants in specific programs. In this section, you identify the sample or population you will be evaluating, identify an evaluation method or tool for each outcome, and include the criteria that will be used with the tool to determine whether the outcome has been met—for example:

- If the tool to measure an outcome is a survey, which questions in the survey are measuring the outcome?
- If the tool is a test, which questions measure the outcome?
- If the tool is an observation, what are the criteria that you apply to the observation in order to identify whether the outcome has been met?

Add limitations of the evaluation method or tool if necessary. Limitations are reminders to you and the reviewer that while the evaluation process may not have gone extremely well, you recognize the limitations and have documented them to be considered in decision making or for improvements to be made the next time. In addition, select other institutional, system or national data (for example, enrollment numbers, faculty-to-student ratios, retention rates, graduation rates, utilization statistics, satisfaction ratings, National Survey of Student Engagement scores) that will be used to help you interpret how and whether the outcome has been met.

Implementation of Assessment Process. This is the planning section for the implementation of the assessment process. Not everything has to be evaluated every year. You can simply evaluate two or three outcomes each year, which will create a multiyear assessment plan, of which the final year of the assessment plan feeds into the comprehensive program review process. Identify who is responsible for doing each step in the evaluation process. Outline the time line for implementation, including the years in which each outcome will be evaluated (so as not to indicate that everything must be evaluated every year). Also include which year you will be reviewing all prior outcomes data results (for example, comprehensive program review year) for a holistic program review discussion.

In addition, identify other programs that are assisting with the evaluation and when they are assisting. Include time lines for external reviewers (including professional accreditation reviews, if applicable) and for communication across departments or colleges. Identify who will be participating in interpreting the data and making recommendations, along with a time line for implementing the decisions and recommendations. Finally, be sure to outline how lines of communication will flow. Who will see the results, when will they see the results, and who will be involved in determining whether the results are acceptable?

Results. Summarize the results for each outcome as well as the process to verify, validate, or authenticate the results. This may include how results were discussed with students, alumni, other program faculty and administrators, or external reviewers. Link the results generated from the outcomes-based assessment results to any other program, college, or institutional performance indicators.

Reflection, Interpretation, Decisions, and Recommendations. This section summarizes the decisions and recommendations made for each outcome and illustrates how you determined if the results were satisfactory. It therefore requires describing the process used to inform how the level of acceptable performance was determined and why it was determined as such.

Illustrate how decisions and recommendations may be contributing to the improvement of higher-level goals and strategic initiatives. Identify the groups that participate in the reflection, interpretation, and discussion of the evidence that led to the recommendations and decisions. It may then be helpful to summarize the suggestions for improving the assessment process, tools, criteria, and outcomes. Finally, be sure to identify when each outcome will be evaluated again (if the outcome is to be retained and who is responsible).

Documentation of Higher-Level Feedback. This section is designed to document how results are used and how the results are disseminated throughout the institution. The intent is to document conversations and collaborations that are being implemented in order to systematically and institutionally improve student learning and development. Include the routing of the recommendations or decisions (for example, who needs to see the recommendations or be involved in the decision making) if resources, policy changes, or other information was required outside the scope of the program. For example, if you are the program coordinator and the decisions you and your students recommend require the approval of the department director, then you need to indicate that the approval of the decision must flow through the departmental director.

Appendixes. Include any appendixes that may help illustrate the manner in which you evaluate your program. For example, you may want to include the curriculum alignment or outcome and delivery map or the tools and criteria to evaluate each outcome. You may also choose to include any external review of the plan, results, or decisions and what was concluded from that external review. Include any budget plans and resource reallocation or allocation documents as well (Bresciani, 2010).

Step Eight: Allocate and Reallocate Resources to Help Realize the Goals. Jenefsky and others (2009) discuss in detail how outcomes-based program review provides an effective way for institutional leadership to use systematically collected data to inform specific decisions for improving strategic plan initiatives. Thus, the findings and recommendations from step 7 can be used as evidence to inform decision-making processes at various levels in the institution (for example, from the program level through the university level).

In order to frame this discussion, remember that some suggestions to improve strategic initiatives can occur with very little resource reallocation (for example, resequencing process steps, refinements in the criteria for student evaluation, or reorganization of workshop material). Other findings may point to a need for a larger reallocation of resources, ranging from staff development for assessment to hiring more staff or faculty members to fill unmet needs.

Step Nine: Make It All Systematic. The final step in this process is to make the entire data-driven planning process systematic. This requires institutional leadership to schedule periodic holistic reviews of their processes in order to ensure that they are working together to inform data-driven planning. There are several things to consider when creating a systematic, sustainable, and data-driven planning process. The first is to build collaborations across departments, colleges and divisions, and hierarchical structures so that information can flow in an environment of trust. Second, review position descriptions and personnel review processes to ensure that faculty and staff are constantly reminded of the importance of engaging in data-driven planning, given professional development opportunities to learn how to do this well, and rewarded for using data to inform decisions. Third, maintain the integrity of the data by being forthright with how data will be used for planning purposes, resource reallocations, and professional development opportunities. Fourth, consistently use data and provide systematic processes for communicating how the data are used for informing decisions and planning. This will motivate faculty and staff engagement in the process. Finally, identify strategies to keep morale high when someone's program is not selected as an institutional priority.

Conclusion

Ensuring these steps are followed will more than likely lead your institution to establishing an effective data-driven planning process. The gathering and analysis of data also has the potential to strengthen the implementation of a well-documented plan. The ongoing cycle of evaluation and assessment will ensure the plan's effectiveness.

References

Banta, T., Jones, E., & Black, K. *Designing Effective Assessment: Principles and Profiles of Good Practice.* San Francisco: Jossey-Bass, 2009.

Bresciani, M. J. *Outcomes-Based Academic and Co-Curricular Program Review: A Compilation of Institutional Good Practices.* Sterling, Va.: Stylus Publishing, 2006.

Bresciani, M. J. "Assessment and Evaluation." In J. Schuh, S. Jones, and S. Harper (eds.), *Student Services: A Handbook for the Profession.* San Francisco: Jossey-Bass, 2010.

Bresciani, M. J., Gardner, M. M., and Hickmott, J. *Demonstrating Student Success in Student Affairs.* Sterling, Va.: Stylus Publishing, 2009.

Bresciani, M. J., Zelna, C. L., & Anderson, J. A. *Assessing Student Learning and Development: A Handbook for Practitioners.* Washington, D.C.: National Association of Student Personnel Administrators, 2004.

Drucker, P. "Managing Knowledge Means Managing Oneself." *Leader to Leader,* 2000, *16,* 8–10.

Fullan, M., and Scott, G. *Turnaround Leadership for Higher Education.* San Francisco: Jossey-Bass, 2009.

Jenefsky, C., and others. *WASC Resource Guide for Outcomes-Based Program Review.* Oakland, Calif.: Western Association of Schools and Colleges, 2009.

Kuh, G. D., and Associates. *Student Success in College: Creating Conditions That Matter.* San Francisco: Jossey-Bass, 2005.

Maki, P. L. *Assessing for Learning: Building a Sustainable Commitment Across the Institution.* Sterling, Va.: Stylus Publishing, 2004.

McClellan, E. "Promoting Outcomes Assessment in Political Science Departments: The Role of Strategic Planning." Paper presented at the annual meeting of the APSA Teaching and Learning Conference Online, Baltimore, 2009. Retrieved May 26, 2009, from http://www.allacademic.com/meta/p11617_index.html.

Reh, F. J. "Key Performance Indicators: How an Organization Defines and Measures Progress Toward Its Goals." 2009. Retrieved July 24, 2009, from http://management.about.com/cs/generalmanagement/a/keyperfindic.htm.

Schuh, J. H., and Associates. *Assessment Methods for Student Affairs.* San Francisco: Jossey-Bass, 2009.

Suskie, L. *Assessing Student Learning: A Common Sense Guide.* (2nd ed.) San Francisco: Jossey-Bass, 2009.

Upcraft, M. L., and Schuh. J. H. *Assessment in Student Affairs: A Guide for Practitioners.* San Francisco: Jossey-Bass, 1996.

Western Association of Schools and Colleges. "Handbook of Accreditation." 2008. Retrieved July 24, 2009, from http://www.wascsenior.org/findit/files/forms/Handbook_of_Accreditation_2008_with_hyperlinks.pdf.

MARILEE J. BRESCIANI is a professor of postsecondary education and codirector of the Center for Educational Leadership, Innovation, and Policy at San Diego State University.

5

An effective strategic planner needs strong financial management skills to implement the plan over time. This chapter discusses how to enhance the effectiveness of a strategic plan through an examination of the purposes and phases of budgeting.

Strategic Planning and Financial Management

James F. Conneely

Strong financial management is a strategy for strategic planning success in student affairs. It is crucial that student affairs professionals understand the necessity of linking their strategic planning with their financial management processes. This process requires them to develop skill sets in financial management as well as in strategic planning and implementation. These skills will ensure a place at the decision-making table during the resource allocation process or, more significant, the resource reallocation process. Making educated decisions about reallocating resources requires a working knowledge of where the resources are and how they are managed. This has become even more crucial as institutions have developed a comprehensive planning process that ties strategic planning and financial management together.

Previous chapters have detailed the importance of values and assessment in driving a successful strategic plan. This chapter looks at financial management in a broad sense, including linking the process to strategic planning. It therefore examines the purpose and phases of financial management, the importance of it in relation to the strategic plan, some basic concepts related to budgeting and strategic planning, how to approach retrenchment and reallocation while staying true to the strategic plan, and, finally, how to develop some better competencies in financial management along with those of strategic planning.

Welsh, Nunez, and Petrosko (2005) write, "Strategic planning is one of the most persuasive and, arguably, most important management

New Directions for Student Services, no. 132, Winter 2010 © Wiley Periodicals, Inc.
Published online in Wiley Online Library (wileyonlinelibrary.com) • DOI: 10.1002/ss.375

activities in higher education at the beginning of the 21st century" (p. 20). They also contend that the need for strategic planning has intensified in higher education because of severe resource constraints, and increased expectations for accountability and strategic planning sets the frame work for decision making.

An effective student affairs strategic planner needs good financial management skills to implement the plan over time. Keller (1997) believes that ignoring the financial realities of university life is one of the most common items of neglect in strategic thinking. There are many definitions of *financial management,* but for the purpose of student affairs and strategic planning, financial management is a comprehensive set of activities involving nearly every institutional officer, directed toward meeting program needs, and achieving long-range institutional health (Vandament, 1989). The role of financial management is to assess risk and resource trends and assist in developing strategies that balance risk and resources in order to fulfill divisional goals (Dickmeyer, 1982). Therefore, a student affairs organization must have a clear and well-developed plan that clarifies strategies to achieve the desired future direction. The best plan can sit on the shelf, but it is securing the funds to achieve it that keeps the plan alive and instills faith in its value among faculty, staff, students, and other stakeholders. A successful strategic planner and implementer needs effective financial management skills to realize the vision and direction set forth. One of the primary roles of professionals in student affairs is to obtain the resources necessary to implement the ideas, programs, and services that students need or desire (Barr, 2002).

Today's students expect their college or university to have in place whatever they need or want. They expect elaborate wellness centers to be fully equipped and never closed. Food courts rivaling those in the most modern shopping malls are a must. Residence halls featuring all of the latest conveniences need to be provided. All of these "necessities" must be provided by colleges and universities in order to compete for the best students (Wettz, 2005). Higher education has to adjust to a changing student population. Facilities and services need to be provided that meet the needs of these students. All of these changes are additional expenses.

Being a Good Financial Manager and Strategic Planner

There are many obvious reasons for being a good financial manager. These include being accountable to the many stakeholders on and off campus, having the necessary resources to meet the needs of constituents, and helping the institution achieve its mission and goals. These are also the same reasons it is important to be a good strategic planner. It is a road map helping to steer the administrator of that particular unit through the year and assist in the planning process itself.

NEW DIRECTIONS FOR STUDENT SERVICES • DOI: 10.1002/ss

In a study conducted by the DRC Group in 2007, student services leadership were being asked to do more with less but also provide resources to those in need. In addition, funding and revenue generation, especially outside the campus, was becoming more of an issue related to their roles as planners and managers. Finally, the ability to track resource use and measure student success was becoming more important as student services leaders were asked to link strategic planning and financial management.

Fain (2009) believes that the lack of sound financial planning creates a misperception about an institution's fiscal health because many colleges and units within the college have become adept at just surviving year to year, without conducting long-term strategic financial planning. Student affairs administrators can promote a strong fiscal health within their division of student affairs by creating a long-term plan rather than just moving about year to year. Additional benefits to being a sound financial manager and effective strategic planner may not be so obvious, but they are important to keep in mind while developing competencies as a student affairs administrator.

Be in Control. Even though one may not enjoy the notion of managing finances or being a strategic manager, it is necessary to do so in order to have an effect on the direction and success of programs. While an individual alone may not affect the resources necessary for all programs, it is still important to understand how an institution works from the financial perspective. Otherwise someone else may dictate all resource decisions. By understanding the intricacies of financial management as a parallel tool in achieving the strategic plan, a student affairs professional will know how to redirect monies, secure additional resources, and be able to collaborate with others to achieve strategic goals.

Have Influence. The old saying, "He who has the gold, has the power," is not far off when it comes to financial management and strategic success at colleges and universities. Many times a student affairs professional who is seeking to achieve a goal may have to justify in a detailed fashion why the funding is needed for a certain program, position, or activity. Often this justification is presented to individuals who do not come from the student development perspective and do not understand how the programs and activities contribute to student success.

Student affairs practitioners who are good financial managers and know how to create revenue to support the strategic plan can influence the direction not only for their areas of responsibility but often for the entire institution. By demonstrating an understanding of how the institution's finances work and are related to the strategic plan, student affairs is at the table and is a voice to be heard at resource allocation (or reallocation) time. Instead of just requesting money, they can develop a strategic plan that includes a financial plan, determine what is needed, and show how the money can be obtained.

Earn Respect and Credibility. A student affairs professional who is a good financial manager and also understands the money side of the institution has an advantage in earning the respect of colleagues in financial affairs. This respect can then translate into being a credible administrator.

Earning this respect does not come easy. Since budgeting or finances may not come naturally to student affairs professionals, hard work, studying, and asking questions are the key. Being diligent and detailed in examining finances and establishing a plan is important. One must understand not just the expense side but also the income side when putting a ledger together. In addition, the assumptions used when establishing planning assumptions related to finances must be accurate and realistic. The quickest way to lose the respect of financial professionals is not to do the homework. Most professionals in financial affairs truly do want to help, and those in student affairs who ask questions will better serve the student affairs strategic plan and the institution.

Be a Collaborator. A more obscure reason for wanting to be a good financial manager and strategic planner in higher education is to serve as a consensus builder or linchpin. Student affairs professionals have not had a strong history as solid financial managers or with understanding the financial areas of higher education. For many years, it has been said that student affairs must build partnerships with academic affairs, and we have done so. Now we need to build those same partnerships with financial affairs. If done well, those two types of collaborations and partnerships can serve student affairs professionals well. Student affairs professionals can develop a place at the resource table by bridging the worlds of academic and financial affairs.

Financial Management and Planning

The components of sound financial management incorporate many aspects associated with a solid strategic planning process. Taken together, the steps necessary to build a comprehensive strategic plan are transferrable to establish a financial plan. "Financial planning requires decisions on major budget drivers, assumptions about rates of increase or decrease of resources, the forecast period (often the same as the strategic plan), and the accuracy and comparability of the data used to drive the analysis" (Chabotar, 2007, p. 1).

Strategic budgeting is defined by its specific linkages to the institution's strategic plan. A strategic budget funds and implements the institution's mission, vision, and core values, and the budget process is organized around the institution's strategic direction and its short-term initiatives. The characteristics associated with a truly strategic financial plan include consistently referring to the mission and values of the institution, clearly distinguishing between continuing and one-time monies, linking the major expenditures to the campus master plan, and explaining the comparative data and benchmarks used in developing the plan (Chabotar, 2007).

Similar to strategic planning models, financial planning models forecast five years or more to detect future implications of current budgets. A key strategic issue that student affairs administrators need to keep in mind when linking their financial plan with the strategic plan is whether existing resources are sufficient to enable them to fulfill its mission (McCarthy and Turner, 1998).

Purpose for Financial Management. The overarching purpose for establishing a financial management plan is the long-term protection and development of the organization's ability to accomplish its mission. In many ways. this is also the purpose of developing a strategic plan. The financial plan needs to complement the provision of adequate resources necessary to support the valued direction and strategies of the organization. It also needs to ensure compatibility with the strategic values and priorities through a clearly articulated process of accountability to those organizational constituencies with a stake in the organization's mission and services.

Evaluating strategic planning efforts consists of at least two steps: the first, discussed in Chapter Four, is to identify the specific strategic indicators that will effectively measure how well you are accomplishing the stated objectives, and the second is assessing whether the plan is on time and on budget (Chabotar, 2006): "A strategic indicator measures organizational performance in a critical decision area and is used to shape, inform, and support policymaking. It connects planning and action, provides concrete targets around which to mobilize enthusiasm and resources, improves accountability for results, and promotes the use of data for decision making" (Chabotar, 2006, p. 45).

Chabotar (2006) believes that five tests or questions are associated with effective strategic indicators:

- Whether the set focuses on issues that matter to the institution
- Whether the indicators should flow from the mission and strategic plan and be used to evaluate progress toward their accomplishment
- Determining whether a reasonable cause-and-effect relationship exists between institutional action and movement in the indicators
- Adopting no more than fifteen to twenty indicators at the executive or top level of analysis
- Regularly reporting progress on the indicators with analysis of data and projections for the future

Five Steps to a Financially Strategic Plan. There are five steps in developing a financial management plan:

1. Identify the needs and priorities of the plan
2. Understand the factors and assumptions used to build the financial model.
3. Determine the span of time of the plan.

4. Implement the plan.
5. Conduct assessment to measure the success of the plan.

Step One: Identify Needs and Priorities. By linking the financial plan with the strategic planning process, needs and priorities for funding should be easily identified. As addressed in Chapter Three, through a strategic plan, a student affairs unit is identifying its purpose as it relates to the mission of the institution, the goals, and the strategic directions necessary to achieve the goals. It is an outline or a format for projecting the needs of the student affairs division and identifying the potential costs associated with fulfilling those needs.

The needs and priorities may be additional staff in the counseling center to handle the increase in mental health issues on campus, new programs to address financial literacy for students to reduce the amount of money they are borrowing, or renovating a residence hall to meet the demands for additional amenities. Whatever they are, the needs and priorities demonstrate it is important to identify the money associated with these items. They should be outlined as one-time monies needed or reoccurring resources needed annually.

Step Two: Understand the Factors and Assumptions. The plan should clearly outline the assumptions or factors that were used in developing it. By highlighting the assumptions and factors specifically, you will be able to take a proactive approach in adjusting your financial plan if the assumptions are not realized or other factors arise that cause the original projections to change. For example, if you as a student affairs administrator are using enrollment projections to justify additional staffing, how will you address the situation if the projections are not realized? Will you give the positions back? Will you reallocate them to meet other needs of the division? Identifying the potential risk as they relate to the assumptions on which you build a budget is important in helping others to understand your decision-making framework.

Other factors are important in the development of a sound financial plan. Depending on the type of institution, legislative and state directives may have to be considered in planning. Tuition increases might be regulated, retirement systems might dedicate the institution's contributions, and whether an institution is self-insured will also contribute to the financial picture. Internally, directives from the board of trustees, equity issues, and safety and security issues may be important to the plan as well. As mentioned in Chapter One, these factors should be identified during the environmental scan of the planning process so they can be part of the development process rather than forcing the student affairs professional to react.

Historical institutional data such as previous budget reports can be beneficial in developing a financial plan, but these are not the only data needed. (Chapter Four details the importance of data from other sources.)

Chabotar (2006) believes the use of benchmarks in establishing key indicators allows administrators to identify comparison groups—current competitors as well as programs one aspires to compete with in academia and other student affairs programs at comparable institutions. KPMG and Prager, Sealy and Co., LLC, has developed the Composite Financial Index for use in financial benchmarking in higher education (Chabotar, 2006). Other benchmarking tools are the Higher Education Price Index, Consumer Price Index, and Educational Benchmarking Incorporated. The most important part of benchmarking is deciding which benchmarks to use. Institutional type, size, geographical location (rural, suburban, urban), size of budget, and cost of living are factors to consider when choosing appropriate benchmarks.

Step Three: Determine the Term of the Plan. Consistent with the strategic planning process, a financial plan is created for both the short term (yearly goals and objectives) and the long term. It must be remembered that the further a plan is carried out, the less accurate it might be down the road. Since financial plans are built on current data and assumptions about the future, those assumptions may not be realized, thus changing the dynamics of the plan. It is wise to build in an inflationary predictor for future costs, but depending on the economy, that percentage may be higher or lower than predicted. Along the same lines, the costs of doing business, such as salaries, fringe benefits, and utilities, may not follow the trends or assumptions that were built into the initial plan and may need to be adjusted. Depending on the type of institution and the sources of funding, state allocations may decrease, endowment returns may not be realized, and investments may be weak, all resulting in a need to adjust the financial plan. Spikes in the economy do occur, but the longer period of time a plan is developed for, the greater the likelihood is that the plan will need to be modified at some point.

Step Four: Implement the Plan. Transparency and openness are keys to successful management of a financial and a strategic plan. It is a living document that needs to be attended to on a regular basis. As with any other financial accountability process, ensuring the accuracy and integrity of the financial plan requires using it as a decision-making tool. As with the strategic plan, going outside the scope of the financial plan could lead to unstable financial conditions for student affairs over the long term.

Where a student affairs organization with a strategic plan puts its resources dictates its priorities. If the financial plan and the strategic plan are not linked and managed together, they can move out of alignment, and one of two consequences may happen. The institution (more important, the president) may lose confidence in the student affairs strategic plan and worry that institutional priorities are not being considered, or the long-term financial health of the division is compromised because there is no longer a road map helping the division to achieve its mission of educating and serving students in a managed and controlled fashion.

NEW DIRECTIONS FOR STUDENT SERVICES • DOI: 10.1002/ss

Step Five: Conduct an Assessment. Chapter Four stressed the importance of assessment when evaluating learning outcomes or the fulfillment
of the strategic plan. It also has a crucial part in determining the success
of a strategic financial plan. Assessing the plan is important, but assessing
the process in building the plan is equally important. Evaluating the
assumptions, the indexes used, and the benchmark data should be done
annually to make sure that they remain appropriate as the plan moves
forward.

Advancing the Strategic Plan When the Fiscal Climate Changes

No campus leader could have predicted the full effect of the financial tur-
moil of recent times. Colleges, or more specifically, divisions of student
affairs with solid strategic plans, are more likely to remain focused and
perhaps even spot opportunities. Planning experts indicate, "If you're really
strategic in your thinking, a crisis like this doesn't throw you" (Fain, 2008,
p. 1).

Major changes do not result in the demise of a student affairs strategic
plan. In fact, this is the time when a strategic plan is of most importance.
The plan identifies the priorities and the articulated values. Fiscal dimin-
ishment often means delaying accomplishments, but it does not mean
abandoning visionary goals or changing direction.

Dealing with Retrenchment and Reallocation of Resources

Part of the process for determining how to manage financial challenges
through retrenchment (the process of reducing expenses) and reallocation
(redirecting resources initially set aside for one purpose to be used for
another) of resources is developing some criteria for reviewing possible
strategic decisions. The development of the criteria should use the strategic
plan as a starting point. One of the unknowns when it comes to financial
management is when things are going to take a turn for the worse, because
sooner or later, they will. Whether it is the economy, unexpected expenditures, a natural or unnatural disaster, or something else, a leader in higher
education at some point will need to make decisions around the retrenchment or reallocation of resources. Some of the same strategies used in
developing the initial strategic and financial plans can be used during the
retrenchment and reallocation process.

Student affairs administrators have seven guidelines to refer to when
looking at retrenchment and reallocation decisions.

First, strong organizations often need retrenchment and reallocation as
much as declining organizations do. As administrators, we sometimes can
be blinded by the success we have on campus in meeting the needs of students. The surveys conducted, positive press in the student newspaper, and
growth in attendance at student programs all point in the direction that

NEW DIRECTIONS FOR STUDENT SERVICES • DOI: 10.1002/ss

things are going well. Doing a thorough assessment of programs and services in student affairs makes it possible to stay ahead of major retrenchment and reallocation by being good stewards of all resources, fiscal and human.

Second, implications for the mission of the division of student affairs should be considered in advance of significant shifts in staff, programs, or services. Decisions outlining potential reductions or reallocation should be compared to the institution's mission. (The hope is that this was fully vetted in the strategic plan.) If a cornerstone of the institution's mission is affordability, then implementing student fees to cover reduction in budgets, and thereby increasing the cost to attend, would not be central to the mission of the institution. When conducting an analysis on what programs (academic or otherwise) and services to reduce or eliminate, each analysis should look not only at the financial aspects but also at how it will affect the institution in carrying out its mission.

Third, retrenchment must consider the possibility of future growth. The life cycles of organizations, including student affairs, often alternate between periods of decline and ones of growth. How a decision influences possible growth opportunities down the road must be vetted. For example, a housing program that is experiencing problems of low occupancy might be inclined to convert the building to an alternate use or sell it back to the institution. In the short term, that decision might be valid, but if occupancy does increase or enrollment needs change, then how will additional growth be handled if a residence hall has been taken off line? The bottom line when making decisions to retrench or reallocate based on usage decline is to determine whether those decisions can be easily reversed if needed.

Fourth, decreasing expenses has a more predictable impact on financial conditions than increasing revenues. Solving fiscal problems by increasing revenues may be less disruptive, but it can be risky. Raising money by increasing housing rates, increasing student fees, or even adding new student fees provides no guarantees. Decreasing expenses is a more predictable way to control finances. Increasing revenue does have a better chance, in the long run, of preserving the division's mission than cutting staff, facilities, and other services on which the mission depends. The goal is to find a balance of new funding opportunities while being effective and efficient with reductions to programs and services.

Fifth, across-the-board reductions should be minimized. These reductions promote shared decision making when they allow department directors considerable discretion about where they make the cuts. If the individuals who helped develop the initial plans are not involved at this juncture, then there will be little buy-in or ownership. All levels of staff can provide insight into how reallocation and retrenchment can happen. Along with being inclusive in the process, communication is vital. Staff members need to understand the severity of the situation. It is not realistic to ask for staff to make good decisions if they are not allowed to have the information necessary to analyze and understand. Holding back information builds a sense of mistrust and lack of confidence that everyone is in this together.

Sixth, more revenues often mean more costs. The total amount of new revenue that could be generated by increasing enrollment or increasing occupancy is not important. What is important is the actual amount realized after related costs are factored in. Recruiting additional students will increase tuition revenue, but it also increases the cost of student services and student aid. Net revenue needs to be examined to determine if there is an actual return on the investment.

Seventh, issues of quality should be described as important in retrenchment as issues of revenue and cost. We all like to think that what we do is the best and of highest quality, but many times they are not where they should be or we want them to be. When budgets tighten, only the strong survive, and that translates into doing away with programs or services that do not add value to the institution at the same level as other initiatives. Quality evaluation needs to take place to ensure that the best return on investment is in place, whether financially or otherwise. Along with quality, the productivity of some programs and services needs to be evaluated.

Conclusion

Competition for students, globalization, cost crunches, and the accountability push from boards, parents, legislators, donors, alumni, and accrediting bodies have all pushed colleges' need for more detailed performance indicators and financial modeling. Many of these same stakeholders have a misperception of their institution's fiscal health because many colleges and units within the colleges have become adept at just surviving year to year. There has been no longer-term strategic financial planning (Fain, 2009).

Strategic planning provides the context for the interrelated decisions that bring the institution and the division of student affairs closer to fulfilling their long-range goals. The strategies implied in the term *strategic planning* refer to conscious attempts to redefine or move the institution, division, or department in a new direction. In addition, financial strategies must answer questions about what these entities will look like financially in five or ten years or more. Financial strategies must reflect the goals and strategies that govern the full strategic plan of the division of student affairs to integrate the financial plans and strategies with the programs, services, and facilities dedicated to the formative curriculum (Dickmeyer, 1982).

References

Barr, M. J. *Academic Administrator's Guide to Budgets and Financial Management.* San Francisco: Jossey-Bass, 2002.

Chabotar, K. J. "Planning and Budgeting for Boards, Chief Executives, and Finance Officers." *Strategic Finance,* 2006, 45–64.

Chabotar, K. J. "Strategic Budgeting." In *Board Basics: Financial Matters.* Washington, D.C.: Association of Governing Boards of Universities and Colleges, 2007.

Dickmeyer, N. "Financial Management and Strategic Planning." In C. Frances (ed.), *Successful Responses to Financial Difficulty.* New Directions for Higher Education, no. 38. San Francisco: Jossey-Bass, 1982.

DRC Group. *The Higher Education Executive Issues Study: Executive Summary Report.* Austin, Tex.: DRC Group, 2007.

Fain, P. "How Colleges Can Keep Strategic Plans on Course in a Stormy Economy." *Chronicle of Higher Education,* Oct. 24, 2008, pp. 1–2.

Fain, P. "Few Governing Boards Engage in Sophisticated Financial Planning, Experts Say." *Chronicle of Higher Education,* May 1, 2009, pp. 1–2.

Keller, G. "Examining What Works in Strategic Planning." In M. W. Peterson and Associates (eds.), *Planning and Managing for a Changing Environment.* San Francisco: Jossey-Bass, 1997.

McCarthy, J. H., and Turner, R. W. "Understanding Financial Statements." In *Board Basics: Financial Matters.* Washington, D.C.: Association of Governing Boards of Colleges and Universities, 1998.

Vandament, W. E. *Managing Money in Higher Education; A Guide to the Financial Process and Effective Participation Within It.* San Francisco: Jossey-Bass, 1989.

Welsh, J. F., Nunez, W. J., and Petrosko, J. "Faculty and Administrative Support for Strategic Planning: A Comparison of Two- and Four-Year Institutions." *Community College Review,* 2005, 32, 20–22.

JAMES F. CONNEELY *is associate provost and vice president for student affairs and associate professor of counseling and educational leadership at Eastern Kentucky University.*

NEW DIRECTIONS FOR STUDENT SERVICES • DOI: 10.1002/ss

This chapter discusses how to involve academic faculty in the student affairs strategic planning process through an understanding of their respective commonalities and the academic view of their work through teaching, scholarship, and service.

Involving Academic Faculty in Developing and Implementing a Strategic Plan

Rich Whitney

Strategic planning is a process that seeks to involve as many internal and external organizational collaborators as possible. For student affairs, this translates into within-divisional work groups and creating opportunities elsewhere on campus. The faculty corps provides a natural partnership to help the division of student affairs create a holistic plan that can have many positive effects for the whole campus (Kezar and Lester, 2009). The diversity of talent, expertise, and perspective available on campus provides energy for powerful partnerships and programs. The key to harnessing this potential energy is understanding the differences and points of view between student affairs and the faculty.

I have had the benefit of working as both a student affairs professional and a faculty member and can offer a unique perspective on involving academics in developing and implementing strategic plans. This chapter explores why student affairs professionals and faculty members should work together to develop and implement a strategic plan. Including faculty in the process can provide additional perspectives, research interests, expertise, as well as committee members and additional energy to complete the process.

After reviewing a general process for implementing a strategic plan, this chapter explores how to include faculty in the process. This partnership provides a more holistic approach and draws on the natural talents and resources waiting to be tapped on campus.

NEW DIRECTIONS FOR STUDENT SERVICES, no. 132, Winter 2010 © Wiley Periodicals, Inc.
Published online in Wiley Online Library (wileyonlinelibrary.com) • DOI: 10.1002/ss.376

Overcoming Culture Clash with Communication

Have you ever tried to explain the functions and duties of student affairs professionals? Family and friends do not always understand this role on campus. Oddly enough, the same can be true for college faculty members. The complexities of the modern university campus for both student affairs and college faculty are unique. The interaction of faculty and staff governance with the learning laboratory of student governance and advising do not typically fit administrative and business models (Kezar and Lester, 2009; Komives and Associates, 2003). Perhaps the fraternity and sorority T-shirt sums up our impasse: "From the outside it is hard to understand, and from the inside it is hard to explain." The campus microcosm can provide just as many internal complexities that can result in a culture clash between the faculty and student affairs professionals (Kezar and Lester, 2009). To make matters more confusing, we have to add to the previous analogy that it is also hard to explain from the inside to the inside. The responsibility of explaining our respective roles and duties on campus lies within each of the divisions of academic affairs and student affairs. There are opportunities for both groups to work together to improve the institution and our final product.

Borrowing from John Gray's book *Men Are from Mars, Women Are from Venus* (1993) to make a point about communication, we can suggest that a similar situation exists between faculty and the division of student affairs. It would seem that just because faculty and student affairs exist on the same campus, each fully understands the other and appreciates the work each contributes to the campus mission and vision. Just as it would be egregious to assume that all men and women fail to communicate, it is also a mistake to assume that all faculty and student affairs professionals are unaware of each group's contributions to the whole. However, there seems to be enough of a divide to make the point that student affairs and faculty do not really understand the contributions one another make to the whole campus approach (Gardner, 1986, 2009; Pace, Blumenreich, and Merkle, 2006; Whitt and others, 2008; Fried, 2007).

Importance of Faculty Involvement

The answer to why faculty should work with student affairs professionals to create and implement a strategic plan involves maximizing talent and expertise, responding to increased competition for funding, increasing the reputation of the university in an increasingly competitive market, and capitalizing on learning efficacy for students.

Many in the community and business world use a university campus as a resource. Faculty members are experts in their fields and research. Within the institution, there is the added benefit of working with these internal experts who already understand the mission, values, institutional history, and culture. It could be easier to attain the sense of collaboration and create a guiding coalition (Kotter, 1996). Often there is a learning curve for both parties while they get up to speed on the culture and history of the organization. That student affairs and faculty exist on the same campus can accelerate the speed of implementation. The benefits to student affairs of working with faculty members include improved relationships and an increased understanding of the expertise that student affairs professionals provide the campus and students.

Student affairs will not be the only beneficiary of this relationship and collaboration. The many offices, services, and programs implemented on campus to help students persist to graduation may be unknown entities in the individual departments of academe. The many resources created by student services may be some of the best-kept secrets on campus outside of the specific program and student populations. This was a surprising fact for me as I was making the transition from the administrative side of campus to the role of professor. This might be explained by the fact that many of the faculty members we encounter during graduate studies in higher education programs work closely with student services and campus offices. This familiarity may seem to be the norm and would be a common assumption that other faculty members are as well versed in campus services and programs.

Where Are We Now?

The reality of the modern university is the competitive market for students. There are increasing options to accomplish educational goals through for-profit campuses, hybrid programs, online options, as well as campuses that combine practical work/life experience with their in-class work and assignments. Students are recruited to a whole campus experience through admissions brochures, campus visits, and student affairs staff. This whole campus approach addresses diversity, classroom ratios, faculty experience, learning opportunities, residence halls, and clubs and organizations, among many others. In short, we present the big picture of campus that incorporates student affairs and faculty functions. Students arrive on campus expecting that same whole campus experience they got excited about when they were deciding where to apply to college. It is vital that academic affairs and student affairs follow through on the promises made at recruitment and tuition collection times (Pace, Blumenreich, and Merkle, 2006; Gardner, 1986, 2009; Newton and Smith, 2008).

Including faculty in the student affairs strategic planning process contributes to the recruiting and persistence of students as well. The current conditions in the higher education market include more competition for funding dollars and a dynamic marketplace in the United States and abroad. Student affairs and the faculty have a stake in working together to create a strategic plan for the benefit of the institution. The efficacy of higher education has been discussed by state and national politicians that could have implications campuswide (Whitt and others, 2008; Pace, Blumenreich, and Merkle, 2006; Newton and Smith, 2008; Dungy, 2005; Komives, 2003; Barr, 2000). We are living in a new era of accountability that requires proving that higher education is delivering a knowledge product that is of value to students and alumni in the job market (Newton and Smith, 2008). There is a perception on the part of some that institutions of higher education are defying authority and resisting accountability (Dungy, 2005) and that we have an inability to provide benchmarks (Newton and Smith, 2008). The organizational links that create the complete college experience for every student happen in a developmental, intentional progression toward the final degree conferral. Each of these functions—recruiting, housing, academics and scholarship, and campus involvement—contributes to the overall student experience. In short, retention and persistence are whole campus concerns that can be addressed through strategic planning.

The differentiation of departments and programs on campus endorses collaboration to the benefit of the student (Newton and Smith, 2008). The more faculty and student affairs can work together to contribute to the quality of education, the better the outcomes will be for our prime stakeholders: our students (Dungy, 2005). Jane Fried (2007) notes that faculty seem to work out of a playbook for teaching separate from another for everything else. She suggests consolidating into one playbook regardless of who has the ball. This passing of the ball is analogous to building relationships and recognizing natural patterns that exist on campus (Askew and Ellis, 2005). Building a better educational experience already exists on campus. By involving faculty in the process, we can improve the experience by streamlining resources, strengths, and expertise (Dungy, 2005). Faculty and student affairs work can be intentional in the delivery of programs, services, and the acquisition of knowledge in the classroom.

Learning efficacy increases in a seamless environment (Whitt and others, 2008; Fried, 2007). Students do not learn in a vacuum, and they do not separate class from participation in student activities or work/life. Transformative and experiential learning incorporates multimodalities of learning (Kolb, 1981; Keeling, 2004, 2006). Learning is a full contact sport. Students learn, and are conditioned to think, through discipline-specific processes they carry with them into clubs and organizations, on-campus interactions, and work/life. There is an existing pattern within the campus approach to learning, which is already integrated (Keeling, 2004, 2006; Fried, 2007). The shift from teaching to learning has been discussed in academy and student affairs publications alike (Association of American Colleges and Universities, 2002; Keeling, 2004, 2006).

Collaborators in Implementing a Strategic Plan

As noted in previous chapters, the process of strategic planning is typically driven by three general questions: Where are we now? Where are we going? and How will we get there? (Askew and Ellis, 2005; Bryson, 1995; Freeman, 2002; Sanders, 1998; Schuh, 2003; Olsen, 2007). To address the first question about current conditions, Chapter Three turned our attention to the institutional mission as a reflection of institutional values. These succinct declarations often provide the values shared throughout campus while honoring the history and founding principles through the perspective of teaching, scholarship, and service. At DePaul University, a discussion with anyone on campus will soon turn toward the mission and values of Vincentian personalism. Other examples of these mission and values are evident in land grant institutions, historically black colleges and universities, and religious or private affiliations. Academic and student affairs staff alike can rally around the common mission and values to create collaboration and camaraderie.

As discussed in Chapter Four, the strategic planning process incorporates a review of principles through an assessment of the environment and the culture as a review and connection to this commonality (Bryson, 1995; Sanders, 1998; Schuh, 2003; Olsen, 2007). Sharing a look at the current conditions helps to focus academic and student affairs staff on the next steps of the strategic planning process. In his book *Leading Change*, John Kotter (1996) posits that common errors to change include complacency, the lack of a guiding coalition, and underestimating the power of vision. Looking at historical and current conditions can help guide where the process will lead.

Given that both student affairs professionals and faculty members are invested in the success of the institution, the importance of faculty involvement in developing and implementing a strategic plan should not be underestimated. Faculty interaction with the division does not have to wait until later phases of the strategic planning process; there could be many opportunities to include faculty earlier in planning and later in the implementation of the plan. This change from strategic planning to management requires a shift in thinking about collaboration and working together. This looks at the incorporation of goals and priorities with execution (Olsen, 2007). The partnerships of student affairs and faculty fostered in the "Where are we now?" and "Where are we going?" will take on a different view at this point. The shift from thinking and planning to making it happen will illustrate where the expertise of student affairs professionals and the faculty starts to coalesce. There can be a struggle of returning to the status quo and the path of least resistance to making the changes part of a new paradigm.

NEW DIRECTIONS FOR STUDENT SERVICES • DOI: 10.1002/ss

What Is Important to Faculty

In order to engage faculty in the process of strategic planning, it is important for student affairs professionals to be aware of the academic triad of teaching, scholarship, and service. Faculty members are constantly evaluating their current and future activities to determine alignment with these tenure and promotion categories (Boice, 2000; Lucas and Murray, 2002). This paradigm seems heightened in the first six years of the traditional tenure-track contract. Student affairs professionals will gain the attention of a faculty member if the suggested collaboration demonstrates an understanding of the professor's world through teaching, scholarship, and service. Make no mistake: the faculty are thinking about it, and it will be noted that the staff member has done his or her homework and has respect for the promotion and tenure process.

Teaching. This seems to be the most visible function of the faculty member on campus. The classroom demeanor and the reputation of a professor are general topics of conversation among students as they negotiate their degree programs. This reputation may spill over in conversations with student affairs staff. Some interaction may occur with the faculty through their subject matter expertise to integrate their knowledge into campus programming and services.

Scholarship. These contributions to the body of knowledge include research, presenting at conferences, writing articles and books, and securing external funding. This aspect of being a professor is generally what initially led many people into doctoral-level training. A faculty member's research trajectory and information dissemination further develop his or her expertise. Depending on the type of institution, the focus between teaching and scholarship may shift between first and second priority. The distinction between primary and secondary could be a very fine line.

Service. It is expected that a faculty member will serve on committees and projects at the department, college, university, field, discipline, and community levels. This bodes well for the division of student affairs in recruiting for help on a strategic planning task force or committee. The list of service opportunities for faculty members seems endless and can easily consume a professor's time and energy. For this reason, the first reaction of many faculty will be to reject participation. But an initial request from the student affairs professional that combines service with opportunities for research or publishing could speed the recruiting process along nicely.

Involving Faculty in the Process

In the following sections, ideas for involving faculty members in the general process of strategic planning are explored with a particular focus on how each aspect of planning can be directly linked to teaching, scholarship, and service. Faculty and student affairs administrators need to work together to sustain and improve their institutions of higher education and meet the needs of students and the scrutiny of external publics (Pace, Blumenreich, and Merkle, 2006; Dungy, 2005; Whitt and others, 2008; Newton and Smith, 2008). The implementation of a student affairs strategic plan will eventually affect most, if not all, areas of campus. Contacting faculty members with research and expertise in complementary areas creates a possible collaboration. In some cases, the faculty member may reach out to inquire about helping or working together. However, it is probably safe to think that faculty will assume the university already has a process or procedure in place. It is a rare occurrence that faculty members are not interested in creating opportunities for additional research, presentations, and publications. The win-win situation for student affairs is depth and breadth for campus initiatives in national journals that could include multiple disciplines. Student affairs should take the lead to invite faculty into their process. At this point, they have the ball.

Step One: Where Are We Now? Very early in the strategic planning process, it would behoove the division to identify additional participants in the process (Askew and Ellis, 2005; Freeman, 2002; Schuh, 2003; Bryson, 1995). Creating an institutional database that identifies the research interests and publication trajectories of the faculty could be a powerful outreach tool for the student affairs division. In many cases, public relations departments maintain a list of campus experts for media and outreach purposes.

Engaging faculty as early as possible could enhance the overall methodologies of the strategic plan (Keeling, Wall, Underhile, and Dungy, 2008?; Creswell, 1994). While this might not be the strength of the student affairs professional, it is one of the skills of the professoriate. Seeking consultation on how to design a research or assessment can would create a useful partnership with faculty members. The anticipated plan could involve existing data or new data collection that could fit qualitative, quantitative, or mixed-methods analyses. At times, the anticipated methods could require data collection from human subjects, which likely would have to be submitted to the institutional review board for approval. Overlooking this detail could jeopardize future publications.

Other aspects the faculty may offer to overall, or subordinate, strategic plans are research questions and a theoretical perspective. A focused research question with a serious analysis of theory and methodology creates operational and productive assessment or research plans (Creswell, 1994; Keeling, Underhile, and Dungy, 2008; Onwugbuzie and Leech, 2006).

This approach to teamwork could model the transformational learning process and provide mutual support for everyone. One article or conference presentation that could emanate here is about the process. An example is from my own association with the campus leadership institute as the faculty scholar. In this situation, the three key staff members (associate vice president, director, and faculty member) all started to keep field notes about the process for potential articles and presentations in the future. Although formal dissemination of these scholarly endeavors may not come to fruition, those early notes and observations would be lost without this foresight. Furthermore, this could result in a lost opportunity for increased communication and collaboration.

Step Two: Where Are We Going? In fact, collaboration is already working in many ways on campus, so the move to focusing on strategic plans is an additional connection. Engaging student affairs partners who are working in such activities as recruiting trips, first-year-experience programs, and orientation would be perfect for members of the strategic planning task force (Gardner, 1986, 2009; Newton and Smith, 2008). Cathy Small (2005), a college professor returning to college to reacquaint herself with her students and get a renewed perspective, provided interesting insights into the potential of collaboration among faculty. In *My Freshman Year* (2005), she posits that faculty need to work with their student affairs counterparts. Finally, the *Beloit Mindset* which describes the 18-year-old's life experiences in comparison to those of us over 30 years old published for the past ten years, is a collaborative effort between a faculty member and a student affairs professional. These and other possibilities for collaboration are more than just having a joint program or combining the programs of two departments into the same event (Newton and Smith, 2008).

Using the faculty talent will require that the student affairs division expand its sphere of influence from traditional higher education administration and student personnel programs. The faculty in these programs are natural resources due to common purpose and a general understanding of student services. But there are other experts who could challenge the division's thinking and add to the larger picture of the strategic plan. Referring to the media experts list to identify business faculty who conduct research on strategic planning, management, and organizational development would yield ideal consultants. Recruiting faculty from psychology or counseling programs to create and lead focus groups and surveys could result in expert facilitation by trained professionals. These disciplines study and train students in the art of facilitation, group dynamics, and group process. This is a natural way of communicating and working with people for those in the helping professions. The editor for the professional journal titled *Specialists in Group Work* may reside on your campus. There may be faculty members who conduct research in the areas of appreciative inquiry that could change the culture of student affairs from, "What do we need to fix?" to celebrating what the division does well. In his book *Good to Great* (2001), Collins calls this appreciation for what an organization does well "hedgehog attributes." This may create an approach that moves the organization from good to great.

Student affairs professionals have done outstanding work in the areas of leadership development. There could be other leadership scholars (for example, in business, history, leadership studies, political science, and public administration) on campus who could help expand this area from the tried-and-true leadership topics and approaches shared at National Association of Student Personnel Administrators and American College Personnel Association conferences. The topic of leadership development has a reciprocal benefit for those same faculty members. By exposing the many disciplines that teach leadership, student affairs could provide those professors with additional resources to be included in their classrooms and assignments. This is a prime example of the integrated learning Fried (2007) suggests in her work. This experiential process could expand the teaching aspects that are so important to faculty members (Keeling, 2004, 2006; Kolb, 1981). The mutual benefits of planning the future of the division will gain momentum through the creation of a coalition and a common vision (Bryson, 1995; Kotter, 1996; Olsen, 2007; Schuh, 2003). This combined planning process creates energy through collaboration and can move the process toward implementation and develop management for change (Bryson, 1995).

Step Three: How Will We Get There? Sustaining change is part of the frustration in implementing the strategic planning process (Bryson, 1995; Freeman, 2002; Kotter, 1996; Olsen, 2007; Schuh, 2003). Executed properly, this process takes time. The discussion about the plan and the goals will be exciting at first. It then has the potential to become monotonous and tedious. Including more partners in the process can help create more buy-in and ownership in the planning, which will lead to stronger programs in the end (Askew and Ellis, 2005). Partnerships between faculty and student affairs can grow organically along the route rather than waiting for later. Recruiting faculty to work with and train student affairs professionals may also be a way to increase morale and energy along the way. Involving accounting and finance faculty will help the division with budgeting and fiscal management, as addressed in Chapter Five. Other areas that could be of benefit to student affairs professionals are marketing, advertising, and public relations. It is important to engage experts who train future industry leaders to assist in the student affairs educational process. Other areas within the college of education might include special education professors to enhance the important work happening in campus disability resource centers.

Returning to the academic triad of teaching, scholarship, and service may also provide some incentives for student affairs professionals. Working with faculty on an assessment or research protocol could result in publications that will record and disseminate the important work happening on campus. These articles can also translate into educational sessions at national and regional conferences. In many cases, the way for student affairs professionals and faculty to attend conferences is through presentations. Recruiting faculty to attend student affairs conferences is another way to develop future partnerships and programs. Faculty members will enjoy expanding their research trajectory and adding to their record for personal and professional reasons.

Mars and Venus Reconsidered

In the same way that couples can improve their communication with one another after they gain insights into how the other thinks, the same can be true of student affairs professionals and faculty members. In order for academics to be truly engaged and involved in developing and implementing a strategic plan alongside their student affairs colleagues, understanding how the other thinks is the first step in creating collaborative relationships.

Recently a faculty colleague and I were discussing a pending research project she was developing with a campus student affairs department. She is an educational sociologist and was excited about the prospect of working with new colleagues in the university. She made a comment that when she referred to the student affairs activities as *extracurricular*, the student affairs professional helped her with the more appropriate term of *cocurricular*. This professor said, "That was a pivotal moment for me," and she went on to explain a textbook example of why the term *cocurricular* was more appropriate. It was an exciting moment to discuss the field of student affairs with a faculty member and for her to explain how student affairs contributes to the learning process.

The landscape of higher education is changing as institutions use strategic planning to refine and coordinate the delivery of programs, services, and academics. Collaboration between academic affairs and student affairs is now essential to survival (Dungy, 2005; Newton and Smith, 2008). Higher education will continue to be driven by volatility, uncertainty, complexity, ambiguity, and increased demands for accountability (Dungy, 2005; Fried, 2007; Gardner, 2004, 2009; Newton and Smith, 2008; Whitt and others, 2008), which suggests the importance of student services strategic planning. It is imperative that institutions deliver on the promises made in their mission statements and recruitment brochures. Sanford (1967) addressed the campus as a whole in addressing the needs of the student when he presented his ideas and theories. He was a faculty member working in his field when he decided to research and write on colleges and college students. He posited that learning was fostered through "teachers" and the "educational community" through challenge and support.

Perhaps it is time to turn that popular theory back on our own campus settings. How can student services challenge faculty colleagues to improve delivery methods? Too much challenge, and we continue to deepen the divide. Not enough of that challenge will result in the status quo and a lack of immediacy. The crux of the dilemma lies in the support. It is about strengthening relationships and fostering communication between Mars and Venus. Powerful partnerships require supporting each other in creating that idyllic environment that improves our cocurricular teaching, our combined scholarship, and our collective service to stakeholders.

References

Askew, P., and Ellis, S. "The Power of Strategic Planning." *NASPA's Leadership Exchange,* 2005, 3(1) 5–8.

Association of American Colleges and Universities. *Greater Expectations.* Washington, D.C.: Association of American Colleges and Universities, 2002.

Barr, M. J., and Associates. *The Handbook of Student Affairs Administration.* (2nd ed.) San Francisco: Jossey-Bass, 2000.

Boice, R. *Advice for New Faculty Members.* Needham Heights, Mass.: Allyn and Bacon, 2000.

Bryson, J. M., *Strategic Planning for Public and Non-Profit Organizations.* San Francisco: Jossey-Bass, 1995.

Collins, J. *Good to Great.* New York: HarperCollins, 2001.

Creswell, J. W. *Research Design: Qualitative and Quantitative Approaches.* Thousand Oaks, Calif.: Sage, 1994.

Dungy, G. J. "Bridging the Gap Between Quality and Accountability: Strategies to Guide Future Planning." *Leadership Exchange,* 2005, 3, 9–13.

Fried, J. "Higher Education's New Playbook: Learning Reconsidered." *About Campus,* 2007, 12(1), 2–7.

Freeman, J. P. "Are You Ready for Strategic Planning?" In *NASPA's NetResults.* Washington, D.C.: National Association of Student Personnel Administrators, 2002.

Gardner, J. N. "Student Affairs and Academic Affairs: Bridging the Gap." *Carolina Review,* Fall 1986, pp. 46–49.

Gardner, J. N. "Reflections on the Need for Collaborations in a Time of Upheaval: Historical Catalysts and Opportunities for Driving Change in the First College Year." Northern Illinois University, DeKalb, Ill. Speech given on September 25,2009.

Gray, J. *Men Are from Mars, Women Are from Venus.* New York: HarperCollins, 1993.

Keeling, R. P. (ed.). *Learning Reconsidered: A Campus-wide Focus on the Student Experience.* Washington, D.C.: American College Personnel Association and National Association of Student Personnel Administrators, 2004.

Keeling, R. P. (ed.). *Learning Reconsidered 2: A Campus-wide Focus on the Student Experience.* Washington, D.C.: , American College Personnel Association, Association of College and University Housing Officers-International, Association of College Unions International, National Association for Campus Activities, National Academic Advising Association, National Association of Student Personnel Administrators, and National Intramural-Recreational Sports Assoication, 2006.

Keeling, R. P., Wall, A. F., Underhile, R., and Dungy, G. J. *Assessment Reconsidered: Institutional Effectiveness for Student Success.* Washington, D.C.: National Association of Student Personnel Administrators, 2008.

Kezar, A. J., and Lester, J. *Organizing Higher Education for Collaboration: A Guide for Campus Leaders.* San Francisco: Jossey-Bass, 2009.

Kolb, D. A. "Learning Styles and Disciplinary Differences." In A. W. Chickering and Associates, *The Modern American College: Responding to the New Realities of Diverse Students and a Changing Society.* San Francisco: Jossey-Bass, 1981.

Komives, S. K., and Associates. *Student Services: A Handbook for the Profession.* (4th ed.) San Francisco: Jossey-Bass, 2003.

Kotter, J. P. *Leading Change.* Boston: Harvard Business School Press, 1996.

Lucas, C. J., and Murray, J. W. Jr. *New Faculty.* (2nd ed.) New York: Palgrave Macmillan, 2002.

Newton, B., and Smith, J. "Steering in the Same Direction: The Importance of Academic and Student Affairs Relationships to Student Success." *College and University,* 2008, *84*(1), 12–18.

Olsen, E. *Strategic Planning for Dummies.* Hoboken, N.J.: Wiley, 2007.

Onwugbuzie, A. J., and Leech, N. L. "Linking Research Questions to Mixed Methods Data Analysis Procedures." Paper presented at the Southwest Educational Research Association, New Orleans, La., Feb. 9–12, 2006.

Pace, D., Blumenreich, K. M., and Merkle, H. B. "Increasing Collaboration Between Student Affairs and Academic Affairs: Application of the Intergroup Dialogue Model." *NASPA Journal,* 2006, *43*(2), 301–315.

Sanders, T. I. *Strategic Thinking and the New Science.* New York: Free Press, 1998.

Sanford, N. *Where Colleges Fail.* San Francisco: Jossey-Bass, 1967.

Schuh, J. H. "Strategic Planning and Finance." In S. Komives and Associates, *Student Services: A Handbook for the Profession.* (4th ed.) San Francisco: Jossey-Bass, 2003.

Small, C. *My Freshman Year.* Ithaca, N.Y.: Cornell University Press, 2005.

Whitt, E. J., and others. "Principles of Good Practice for Academic and Student Affairs Partnership Programs." *Journal of College Student Development,* 2008, *49*(3), 235–249.

RICH WHITNEY *is an assistant professor in the Department of Counseling and Special Education's college student development program at DePaul University.*

NEW DIRECTIONS FOR STUDENT SERVICES • DOI: 10.1002/ss

7

This chapter describes the strategic thinking, process, and development of Tulane University's Renewal Plan, which was created in response to Hurricane Katrina.

Strategic Planning: Renewal and Redesign During Turbulent Times

Cynthia Cherrey, Evette Castillo Clark

> I have passed through the flood, and I have found power in the water.
> Helen Jaksch, graduate of the "Katrina class" and
> 2009 Tulane Commencement student speaker

In August 2005, Hurricane Katrina, the worst natural disaster in the history of the United States, forced the fall semester closure of Tulane University in New Orleans, Louisiana. In the aftermath of this unprecedented storm, the Tulane leadership set forth a plan for renewal to secure the survival, recovery, and sustainability of the institution, which propelled the campus community into mission-critical focus. The university's historic reopening was in January 2006.

Due to the effects and scope of the disaster, Tulane experienced a magnitude of loss, organizational restructuring, elimination of some programs and units, and change at all staffing and departmental levels. Consequently, the existing student affairs strategic plan, initiatives, and goals necessitated review and realignment with the current renewal plan. Determined to find opportunity in the face of adversity and turbulent times, Tulane University and the division of student affairs reset its course, looking at the sustainability of academic programs, redesigning colleges, exploring new ways of conducting services and programs, and reviewing and strengthening the mission of the campus, which "in an era of declining resources and increasing demands, the mission of an institution can serve as a beacon to guide

NEW DIRECTIONS FOR STUDENT SERVICES, no. 132, Winter 2010 © Wiley Periodicals, Inc.
Published online in Wiley Online Library (wileyonlinelibrary.com) • DOI: 10.1002/ss.377

institutional managers" (Hirt, 2009, p. 20). With renewed purpose and mission in mind, we asked ourselves, *How must we be different to survive? What significant changes need to be made?* Toward this end, the division of student affairs at Tulane had to address transformed services and programs as a complement to the major elements of the renewal plan through a revised division of student affairs strategic plan.

The Tulane Renewal Plan

Given the great loss within the university and in the city of New Orleans, Tulane had no choice but to evolve as a response to Hurricane Katrina. The Tulane Renewal Plan reflects a university that understands the importance of its relationship with the city and its rebuilding efforts. The renewal plan states, "With every devastation visited by nature, there is always a corresponding rebirth" (Tulane University, 2005b, p. 27). What this meant for the university was to create a more financially viable institution, remain true to the long-term goals of the university, advance Tulane's status in higher education, maximize efficiency, and strengthen ties to and support of the city of New Orleans. In doing so, the university's board of administrators approved a sweeping plan that strengthens and focuses the university's academic mission while strategically addressing its current and future operations in the post-Katrina era. The renewal plan achieves two major goals for the university at a pivotal moment in its history: strengthening its commitment to building a world-class educational and research institution and implementing measures to ensure the University's financial stability (Tulane University, 2005a).

The Tulane Renewal Plan was developed with input from a blue ribbon group of internal and external advisors and experts, including Tulane's board, the president's faculty advisory committee, and top administrators from several of the nation's top academic institutions and educational foundations. The strategic road map had Tulane administrators, the Tulane board, and outside consultants responsible for each component. The final plan was presented to and voted on by the Tulane Board of Administrators.

The core of the Tulane Renewal Plan emphasizes the holistic development of all students and an enhanced and distinctive Tulane undergraduate, graduate, and professional student experience that is more "campus- and student-centric" (Tulane University, 2005b, p. 1). The renewed Tulane is defined by characteristics of providing world-class educational and research programs, having a unique relationship to the culturally rich and diverse city of New Orleans, gaining historical strength and ability to strategically redefine itself in light of an unprecedented natural disaster, and possessing financial strength and vitality. For the overall renewal, Tulane would concentrate on limited yet more focused and quality programs and services for undergraduates. Tulane would enhance the value of the collegiate experience for professional students by expanding public service opportunities, cocurricular activities, and, as needed, the curriculum. Finally, Tulane would focus on graduate and research programs in which it has emerging areas of demonstrated expertise and provide distinctive and robust experiences for graduate students. Based on these premises, several major initiatives ensued.

First, Tulane has encouraged its students to develop a commitment to community outreach and public service (service-learning) through the creation of the Center for Public Service. Second, it created a single undergraduate college, Newcomb-Tulane Undergraduate College, which will support and coordinate undergraduate initiatives, simplify the undergraduate academic organization, and consolidate the administrative structure that supports undergraduate education. The Center for Academic Advising was established to replace the current school-based advising system, centralizing services and creating educational plans in line with students' individual objectives. Finally, University College was renamed the School of Continuing Studies in order to recognize its traditional role as the university's primary outreach vehicle serving the general population of New Orleans and online education. Given these university-wide changes, the division of student affairs was prepared to act and assist in redefining the future of Tulane. To date, the Tulane Renewal Plan is used as the university's strategic plan; the division of student affairs uses this document as the foundation for its strategic plan.

The Response of Student Affairs to the Tulane Renewal Plan

Faced with the extraordinary challenges from Hurricane Katrina, the university had to become more strategically focused on and attentive to its mission, which meant that every area, including student affairs, needed to immediately review departments, programs, and overall operations to determine its criticality to the larger university mission. As a result, in student affairs, the Department of English as a Second Language was eliminated, and several departments within student affairs had to operate with minimal staff. With things not exactly the same as they used to be, everything student affairs did now was considered the "new normal." Consequently the student affairs five-point plan (not to be confused with the revised division of student affairs strategic plan) was developed as an immediate response to support the Tulane Renewal Plan with governing principles of supporting more leadership and civic engagement opportunities and building stronger, more meaningful communities. The student affairs five-point plan was developed to have an immediate impact on transition programs and services for the students returning to campus.

Student Affairs Five-Point Plan. Although New Orleans was struggling to come back, we needed to ensure that Tulane students had as normal a collegial experience as possible. This had to be done with limited resources and staffing, so we concentrated our efforts in five critical areas: community service, student leadership, diversity education, residential life, and the "new normal" programming initiatives, which included, for example, Orientation déjà vu, town hall meetings to address the changes occurring at Tulane, a university-wide celebration called "Take TU" to kick off the new year, and events to acknowledge Katrina such as the Katrina tapestry honoring the universities and colleges that took in Tulane students. We were deluged with offers of help from around the world along with our own students' desires to volunteer. Student affairs had to ramp up to meet the community service demand. Race relations were brought to the surface during Hurricane Katrina that student affairs needed to address through education and outreach. Finally, housing needed to be addressed—not only the normal operations and day-to-day of residential life, but also working through the difficulties of students who had lost their belongings in the residence halls and concerning ourselves with staffing up and programming for a cruise ship that was used for additional housing.

The student affairs five-point plan was the bridge between the former student affairs strategic plan and our revised plan that mirrored the Tulane Renewal Plan. With a renewed sense of direction, the division resumed the strategic planning process, which best describes student affairs today and the plans for Tulane's future.

Strategic Initiatives as Broad Themes for Strategic Goals. What came out of the discussion processes, as a result of the revised student affairs strategic plan, were more finely tuned themes that we knew all constituents would have stakeholdership in and that supported the following larger tenets of the Tulane Renewal Plan: The renewed Tulane would be defined by:

- Its world-class educational and research programs
- Its unique relationship to the culturally rich and diverse city of New Orleans
- The university's historical strengths and ability to strategically redefine itself in light of an unprecedented natural disaster in ways that will benefit the Tulane community, New Orleans, and other communities around the globe
- Its financial strength and vitality (Tulane University, 2005b)

The student affairs strategic themes, essentially coined as four strategic initiatives, are consistent with and complement the Tulane Renewal Plan as well as the university's previous strategic plan. Each initiative has implications for every department within student affairs. These four strategic initiatives, based on student affairs as student centered and learning focused, have been developed to build on strengths, address weaknesses, and leverage future growth:

NEW DIRECTIONS FOR STUDENT SERVICES • DOI: 10.1002/ss

Strategic Initiative 1: Student Learning in Multiple Contexts
Strategic Initiative 2: A Distinctive Student Experience
Strategic Initiative 3: A Culture of Service: Staff Accountability and Student Responsibility
Strategic Initiative 4: Developing Staff as Leaders and Educators in the Learning Process

Every year since the university's reopening in January 2006, student affairs develops specific goals that can be categorized under one of the broader strategic initiatives. The success of these goals depends on the relationships we nurture with our many partners on and off the Tulane campus: students, faculty, staff, alumni, parents, and families, as well as groups from the local, national, and international communities.

Implementing the Revised Strategic Plan

A significant personnel change was first made by the vice president for student affairs during Tulane's reopening and alongside the initial process of revising the student affairs strategic plan. An assistant dean of students for divisional planning, a new senior-level position, was created to oversee strategic planning efforts and ensure that goals and actions corroborated the Tulane Renewal Plan. Initially this position worked closely with the associate vice president for university services who was originally tasked with strategic planning; over time, the new assistant dean of students helped lead strategic planning efforts. In this role, the staff member forecasts and plans the strategic direction with the vice president for student affairs, coordinates and monitors all strategic activities, rewrites plans, conducts research as needed, facilitates meetings, plans retreats, oversees communications and trainings, consults on assessment projects, and serves as liaison to the chairs and leads of the committees.

Some critics may view casting the net widely to gather information, feedback, and perspectives for divisional planning processes as time-consuming and constraining. However, spending the time including different voices and developing a rich process with key stakeholders creates a rewarding and effective strategic plan that is central to its implementation. In addition, with regard to student needs, a recent report from the Education Advisory Board notes that providing the opportunity to express concerns and ideas "advances strategic planning leaders' understanding of student needs and helps them better understand the complexity of issues students face" (2009, p. 3). Furthermore, partnerships, purposeful collaborations, and consortiums, for example, were arguably necessary strategies to employ given our campus community experience and direction of renewal. For us, this meant creating "partners in learning" (Miser and Cherrey, 2009, p. 615) for the process of renewal, looking broadly across the university, within our communities and professional associations, and

NEW DIRECTIONS FOR STUDENT SERVICES • DOI: 10.1002/ss

within the city of New Orleans. With an environmental scan, getting input from colleagues as well as students, and looking at potential partners as a first step, we were well poised to address the most critical and concerning issues; we could get ahead of and better prepare for major changes within the university and in student affairs, for example, student demographic changes or increased enrollment for a two-year residential campus; and finally, we could seek resource support or collaboration on projects that were meaningful to the university's renewal. Most notable, and somewhat inherent to our process, was the fortuitous development of our student affairs core community values, developed as a result of revision conversations of our strategic plan. Were it not for open dialogue, feedback, and communication about the strategic plan, our shared values of care, learning, excellence, and accountability and responsibility would not have been adopted so genuinely or so quickly.

Chair and Lead Roles. Senior leaders of the division appoint the leadership within student affairs who will move initiatives and goals forward. All staff members at any professional level within student affairs are considered for a chair role with the intention that they have a strong attachment to and investment in the strategic goal as a part of their everyday professional position. For example, an alcohol education initiative might best be chaired by a staff member overseeing that specific area. Chairs of committees invite membership from across the institution to serve, revise charges and direction of strategic goals as needed, and meet regularly with their committee to shape and implement outcomes. Leads are members of the student affairs senior leadership team who also have a vested interest in the specific goal. They offer overall direction, guidance, and consultation for the chair; help support and cultivate resources; and set the tone and message for committee members in envisioning and embracing the value in which the strategic goal was created.

Communications. Good and frequent communications about the strategic plan, initiatives, goals, and its major players can improve strategic processes. One of the first steps that student affairs facilitated at the onset of the institution's reopening was a PowerPoint presentation entitled, "Strategic Roadshow 101," which was offered at various subdivision staff meetings to begin the basic conversations about thinking, visioning, and planning strategically, thus priming members of the division to consider new directions in student affairs in light of the Tulane Renewal Plan. As the revised plan came to life, the full strategic plan, initiatives, goals, and strategic leadership were uploaded to the student affairs Web site. A printed version of the student affairs strategic plan was made available for distribution for such activities as recruitment, fundraising, student leadership, and broader university-wide committees. Finally, the use of technology was helpful for communicating with strategic leaders. Blackboard, a software that the institution uses for course management, organization communications, document repository, and managing online

NEW DIRECTIONS FOR STUDENT SERVICES • DOI: 10.1002/ss

communities, became fundamental for organizing and communicating the regular activities and projects of each strategic goal. The communication of our work provides for additional considerations and unintended consequences that we may miss in early planning stages, shows our contribution to university renewal efforts, and more substantially, tells our student affairs story.

Processes. Consistent and purposeful meetings and retreats are a major part of strategic planning. Unfortunately, too many of these might create burnout and apathy if they are not coordinated with intentionality, the context of the institutional climate, and understanding of timing in the year, the organizational culture, and staff members' workload. Albeit it is difficult to stay on the pulse of all colleagues' schedules, there is an advantage to mapping out, in advance of the academic year, meeting times for strategic dialogue among colleagues. In addition to committee meetings, leaders are held accountable for providing updates at quarterly divisional meetings attended by mid- and senior-level managers of student affairs (this is encouraged to be as creative and interactive as possible, for example, providing feedback at topical strategic roundtables), one senior leadership team meeting during the year, and an all-strategic-chairs meeting twice a year.

Progress and final reports are an important part of the process, as well as for documentation and history. Assessment of specific objectives within strategic goals is a vital process that is of increasing importance, especially in light of the accountability movement (Mallory and Clement, 2009) and reaccreditation efforts. Consultation on assessment projects and methods is also led by the assistant dean of students for divisional planning. With assessments in place and results to share, student affairs at Tulane University closes the academic year with a summary of every strategic goal and a discussion with senior leadership whether that goal should continue as a priority for the following academic year, move to an established initiative (ownership) to be placed under a department, or be tabled for discussion in a future academic year.

Recommendations for Strategic Planning in Institutional Renewal

In turbulent times, university leadership must respond quickly and adeptly to the possibilities of renewal or redesign of mission and goals. Following is a summary of strategies and recommendations for student affairs leaders and their institutions in which immediate realignment is needed when university plans and goals are dramatically altered:

- *Revise student affairs strategic goals to align with renewed university purposes.* After the successful reopening of Tulane University in spring 2006, this was an opportunity for student affairs to be

New Directions for Student Services • DOI: 10.1002/ss

focused sharply on goals and projects that would have an impact on rebuilding of campus and surrounding community, as well as throughout the city of New Orleans. At every professional level and with as much student input as possible given their various scattered locations after the storm, we engaged in discussions and conducted an environmental scan to get at what mattered most to our fragile community. The alignment of student affairs with revised university purposes fostered the ability to think and plan strategically with a sense of renewed energy and enthusiasm toward new commitments, resources, and partnerships that would serve to maximize learning and development in our communities (Askew and Ellis, 2005; Tulane University, 2005b).

- *View strategic planning as an opportunity to reinvent student affairs.* The revision of the student affairs strategic plan gave us the unique opportunity to review existing programs, services, and initiatives with the purpose of realigning to a larger historical cause: transformation and rebuilding. It also gave us the opportunity to reprioritize and reinvent student affairs to be more student centered and learning focused, better linking students to distinctive experiences only at Tulane, only in New Orleans. Although the mission and vision statements of student affairs altered slightly as a result of the renewal, what in fact did transpire as a result of our new strategic initiatives was the development of student affairs' values statements, which give us an identity and shared philosophy to uphold, and a commitment to stronger assessment of student learning outcomes for each department.
- *Everyone must visualize their investment and generate buy-in.* Probably the hardest yet most important aspect to do, as with any other strategic plan, is to seek investment and buy-in from student affairs colleagues toward a unified direction, set of goals, and initiatives. Schuh (1996) states, "Getting people to accept the plan and begin work toward implementing it will require deliberate, ongoing efforts. Simply assuming people will accept the plan because you say they should is an exercise in wishful thinking" (p. 464). Especially when working toward realignment of student affairs goals to modified university goals, colleague input is greatly needed from every perspective in order to put forth and adopt a plan that everyone can commit to for several years out. They must visualize themselves in the plan, making it part of their day-to-day work in order for action to occur. Ultimately the implementation piece of the plan will have the investment, buy-in, innovation, and energy needed to advance initiatives.
- *Communicate the new goals and initiatives as widely as possible.* The entire student affairs strategic planning process at Tulane University was designed as a major role for one senior staff member to oversee.

All strategic activities, such as meetings, communications, trainings, and reports, to name a few, fell under their direction. Given the university's renewal and reorganization, the immediate widespread communication of new goals and initiatives to the campus community was important. To communicate new initiatives, the entire strategic plan, goals, and chair or lead names and contact information were uploaded to the Web site. Strategic initiatives were printed on promotional items such as mouse pads, mugs, and jump drives, which served both a communication purpose and a gift for colleagues in the division. Staff and faculty outside student affairs were involved members of strategic committees. Quarterly divisional leadership team meetings were hosted where action items and updates are shared by chairs. In addition, formal reports are made to the senior leadership team to get input on next steps. Each academic year ends with a summer retreat with the mid- and senior-level professionals within student affairs and a summary of every strategic goal and its direction for the following year. In this manner, knowing and understanding the strategic plan does not become something that the division hears about only two or three times a year; rather, it is a constant and ongoing communication that makes a point for colleagues to view the plan as part of their day-to-day work.

- *Encourage optimistic thinking and problem solving during institutional fragility.* In uncertain times, especially when a university undergoes repurposing and reorganizing on a major level, staff in student affairs may experience latent doubt, stress, fatigue, and fear. It is important to first recognize that the impact of any major crisis or disaster has lasting effects on personal lives. Encouraging optimistic thinking in light of challenges is helpful even during the most discouraging and unsettling of situations. To do so, one helpful strategy is to seek out staff members who are strong at galvanizing others into action and can share positive attitudes and outlooks with colleagues. These staff members can complement strategic work during difficult times as forward thinkers, seeing the big picture, exploring possibilities, solving problems, assessing with good judgment, and never forgetting that students are the center of our work. In hiring essential new staff, look for professionals who have the ability to adapt to the changing environment, are excited about change, and are creative in their thinking. During institutional fragility, these characteristics affect good decision making for the campus at large.
- *Expect the unexpected.* Strategic planning during times of crisis is like building the ship at sea during a hurricane. Moving quickly and confidently is a requirement for planning and implementation. The crisis gave us a blank canvas. Planning for the future when little is

known about the present is challenging; planning for the unexpected was the norm during Hurricane Katrina. Experimentation and innovation, not perfection, were rewarded. The capacity to expect the unexpected and translate that into our renewal efforts and planning process was valued as we planned for the future.

Conclusion

Through strategic planning in turbulent times, student affairs has unique vantage points, talent, and capabilities to widely influence and affect the priority-setting and decision-making processes of an institution (Askew and Ellis, 2005) and "to assist the members of the campus community to move through challenging times in their history" (Miser and Cherrey, 2009, p. 615). As an alternative to strategic planning, the Tulane Renewal Plan remains premier document of the division of student affairs that focuses our attention from year to year.

In 2005, Tulane University went from survival to recovery in the wake of Hurricane Katrina, and through many processes and revisions, we aligned our student affairs goals accordingly to address how we would respond to and complement this historic renewal. Since 2005, Tulane University reviews its potential and opportunities after the storm and takes another look at its position academically, administratively, and financially to sustain the institution. Given the time spent on creating a regular strategic process and time line, the involvement and investment of many stakeholders, including staff members and students, to shape goals, and the transparency and flexibility in which we conduct our strategic work, student affairs is well positioned to respond to any future, substantive institutional renewal.

References

Askew, P., and Ellis, S. "The Power of Strategic Planning." *NASPA's Leadership Exchange,* 2005, 3(1), 5–8.

Education Advisory Board. "Collecting and Incorporating Student Input into the Strategic Planning Process: Custom Research brief, Apr. 17, 2009.

Hirt, J. B. "The Importance of Institutional Mission." In G. S. McClellan and Associates, *The Handbook of Student Affairs Administration.* (3rd ed.) San Francisco: Jossey-Bass, 2009.

Jaksch, H. Tulane University commencement speech, May 16, 2009.

Mallory, S. L., and Clement, L. M. "Accountability." In G. S. McClellan and Associates, *The Handbook of Student Affairs Administration.* (3rd ed.) San Francisco: Jossey-Bass, 2009.

Miser, K., and Cherrey, C. "Responding to Campus Crisis." In G. S. McClellan and Associates, *The Handbook of Student Affairs Administration.* (3rd ed.) San Francisco: Jossey-Bass, 2009.

Schuh, J. H. "Planning and Finance." In S. R. Komives and D. B. Woodard (eds.), *Student Services: A Handbook for the Profession.* (3rd ed.) San Francisco: Jossey-Bass, 1996.

Tulane University. "Survival to Renewal." 2005a. Retrieved May 10, 2009, from http://renewal.tulane.edu/background.shtml.

Tulane University. "Tulane University—A Plan for Renewal." Dec. 2005b. Retrieved May 10, 2009, from http://renewal.tulane.edu/renewalplan.pdf.

CYNTHIA CHERREY is the former vice president for student affairs at Tulane University and current vice president for student affairs at Princeton University.

EVETTE CASTILLO CLARK is the assistant dean of students at Tulane University.

NEW DIRECTIONS FOR STUDENT SERVICES • DOI: 10.1002/ss

8

*This concluding chapter provides an example of one
institution's strategic plan: mission, vision, values,
measured accomplishments, and future goals. The plan
was written in 2002 with a five-year time line. Thus, it is
possible to assess the results of strategic planning in
student affairs.*

But Does It Really Work? A Vision for Student Services, 2002–2007

Shannon E. Ellis

Unless public colleges and universities become the architects of change, they
will be its victims. In a rapidly changing world, we must build on our legacy
of responsiveness and relevance.

Returning to Our Roots: The Student Experience, Kellogg Commission
Report

This chapter provides a sample of a strategic planning document that is
focused on telling a story to bring the themes, accomplishments, and future
goals to life. The Division of Student Services at the University of Nevada,
Reno wrote the plan in 2002 with annual updates and revisions each year
since then. It illustrates many of the practices and process steps detailed in
Chapter One.

To determine if strategic planning works, consider the university's
165,000-square-foot student union in the new center of campus, two new
residence halls with a new dining commons, a doubling of enrolled Pell
recipients, reduced time to degree, twice increased admission standards,
higher retention and graduation rates, recipient of a McNair Scholars
Grant, and the presence of more than 25 percent students of color in the
freshman class, just to name a few of our aspirations from 2002. These
accomplishments were achieved through a community of student services
professionals who are inspired to move in one direction with the flexibility
to seize opportunities along the way.

New Directions for Student Services, no. 132, Winter 2010 © Wiley Periodicals, Inc.
Published online in Wiley Online Library (wileyonlinelibrary.com) • DOI: 10.1002/ss.378

Student Days at the University of Nevada, Reno, in 2007

It is another sunny start to a day in the year 2007 at the University of Nevada, Reno. Raoul, an international graduate student in biochemistry, jumps out of bed to go back to his lab to initiate a new phase of his research project. He hurries to catch the 7:15 A.M. university shuttle that stops every morning at the entrance of the Graduate/Adult Village adjacent to the campus. If he makes the shuttle, Raoul will be able to stop by the union to buy the commuter student grab-and-go breakfast with a simple swipe of his student ID.

Across campus, Tony, a new student from Las Vegas, is one of 2,108 residence hall students (40 percent from southern Nevada) getting ready for class. This large number of students from southern Nevada demonstrates the state-wide call for the university to better meet the needs of Nevada's citizens. Tony knows demand for space is high, so he is lucky to be living in the hall. Data shared with him by the Freshmen Connections Program to reach out and retain new students clearly show that living in the halls greatly increases academic success and shortens time to graduation. Tony was worried he might not be able to afford a room in the residence halls, but the return of the University Inn on-campus hotel to residential life and housing has helped stabilize rents.

Tony begins his day by turning on his electronic tablet. Midterms begin next week, and Tony is beginning to think strategically about maximizing his grade point average. He logs on to his campus portal where he can access his current class schedule, transcripts, Degree Audit Reporting System report, and financial aid application status.

Tony's placement, financial aid, transcript, and grade book data are also linked to other campus services. He is a first-generation low-income student and is carrying sixteen units this semester. All of these factors were weighed in prioritizing the presentation of support and service options on Tony's portal. He received specific invitations to take advantage of online and campus-based academic support programs, especially tutoring. Freshmen Connections was a great start. Tony's older brother came to Nevada last year after two years at a community college. He made a smooth transition with the help of the transfer center's services.

On his way out the door, Tony waves at Marcy as she boards the shuttle outside the "New/New" Residence Hall. Marcy is excited about attending a book signing on the upper level of the Associated Students of the University of Nevada Bookstore in the new union. As she leaves the shuttle at the gateway entrance to campus, Marcy admires the new student union and library nestled together on a hillside. Since Marcy is president of the Multicultural Student Alliance, she stops by the club's office in the union's multicultural student resource center. She wants to see what student film is showing tomorrow night in the union's two-hundred-person movie theater. She has just enough time to get a smoothie at the union's Los Lobos

NEW DIRECTIONS FOR STUDENT SERVICES • DOI: 10.1002/ss

coffeehouse. Marcy walks by an atrium that connects the union to the library and to Lombardi Recreation Center.

Inspired by the book signing, Marcy turns on her laptop and logs in to her portal. Early in her academic career, Marcy was prompted to fill out an informal career interest inventory on her portal. Because she did, she made an early connection with both virtual and real career counselors who have helped her develop a career path. She passes the Student Services Assessment Office. The university has become a model across the nation on the implementation of state-of-the-art assessment practices, particularly in terms of illustrating the active use of assessment findings to guide decision making. Ongoing assessment by all student services professionals applied to learner-centered issues has resulted in more funding for effective programs.

Across the city, Mya Hernandez steps out of The Limited at Meadowood Mall with her mother. They walk over to the kiosk labeled "University of Nevada." She has been meaning to contact the university to see whether she qualifies for admission, but she is always too busy and does not know where to start. By simply touching the screen, a DARS report shows that she needs one additional science class. While she is on the Web, she decides to request more information about the university (in Spanish and English) as well as set up a tour on campus next week. The University of Nevada has come to be known as the school of choice for students of color who find a challenging yet supportive environment for their learning.

Tony joins up with Marcy to sit in on an alcohol peer education workshop. The classroom in the residence hall is not being used by an academic department tonight, so they have a big space for learning. He remembers an article he saw in today's *Sagebrush* campus newspaper about a joint student services/academic affairs "retention and persistence" focus. He sees the awards hung on the wall that recognize the continued success of this partnership on such issues as diversity and leadership.

Another day begins to wind down for these students. As Raoul works tirelessly in his lab, Mya sits at home and motivates herself to study so that she can realize her dream of attending the university.

Realizing the Vision

The seven strategic themes reflected in this story emerged from the student services planning efforts in 2001–2002:

- Enrollment/access and opportunity
- Retention and persistence
- Graduate students
- Residential community
- Student union
- Assessment
- Technology

Every department committed to working on each theme as part of its annual goal-setting and work plans. In addition, it was determined that strategic implementation teams would be developed to carry out the initiatives around each theme over the next five years. Team chairs were selected given their interests, talents, and, most of all, areas of responsibility. The theme was directly related to their job, and more than anyone else, they were committed to achieving the goal.

The strategic implementation teams began their work in late spring 2002 by revising their charges, establishing baseline key performance indicators, and setting annual goals for the key performance indicators (KPIs) up to 2007. The June 2002 student services annual retreat highlighted team "reports from the future" to update and involve student services staff in the work being achieved on our strategic themes. The strategic implementation team leaders met as a group every two weeks until the first of September. They now meet monthly. The leaders are coordinated by the vice president of student services. Meetings focus on reports of accomplishments, finding collaborative areas of work across teams, and solving problems encountered in trying to achieve the necessary results. Retreat and division meetings focus on updating staff on progress made on the strategic plan.

All department and individual goals for 2002 focused on achieving the seven themes in the strategic plan, and these are reviewed and evaluated on an ongoing basis. In the fall of 2002, all departments reviewed and updated their fall 2001 phase I plans with particular attention to trends, strengths, and weaknesses and future initiatives. The student services leadership shared and discussed the strategic plan with representatives of the Associated Students of the University of Nevada and Graduate Student Association (GSA) to discuss mutual progress and future direction. We sought to understand and complement one another's plans. Our success in this area is reflected in this chapter.

All interested individuals were invited to share their viewpoints, perspectives, and ideas throughout the year, especially during the preparation of this document. The overall strategic efforts by the student services division continued to be unified by five core values identified in year 2000. These essential and enduring tenets are as follows: pursuit of knowledge, fostering diversity, ensuring quality, creating a safe environment, and maintaining a clear vision.

Student Services Accomplishments and 2003 Goals

The following sections summarize the strategic implementation team and student services department achievements and future goals around the seven strategic themes.

NEW DIRECTIONS FOR STUDENT SERVICES • DOI: 10.1002/ss

Theme One: Enrollment/Access and Opportunity

We are committed to future enrollment growth that balances academic preparation, motivation and access. We will continue to recruit the best and brightest students with an enrollment plan which focuses on access and opportunity. We will increase statewide outreach to middle schools and expand recruitment in Southern Nevada. We will strengthen our Transfer Center in an effort to help students start their education at a Nevada Community College and transfer to the University.

Accomplishments. A review of these KPIs demonstrates success in areas set forth in our strategic plan. The university realized a 6.9 percent increase in new freshmen in fall 2002. The academic profile of this group increased to a mean high school GPA of 3.36, the highest in the history of the university. In realizing a 15.2 percent increase in students of color in fall 2002, the university reached 98.4 percent of its 2005 goal for number of students of color. A new diversity recruitment plan was developed with the assistance of community leaders of color on and off campus. It sets a goal of 25 percent of the university's undergraduate population to be students of color by 2011.

Outreach efforts were strengthened this past year in several ways:

- Enrollment services led in the development of an aggressive diversity recruitment plan that was shaped and shared with numerous educational and cultural groups on campus and in the community.
- Spring and fall meetings were conducted by the Office of the Vice President of Student Services regarding increasing access with key members of business, industry, and the community in Washoe County, as well as specific student groups on campus.
- Ties were developed by a variety of Student Services departments with the P-16 Washoe Educational Collaborative in pursuing specific outreach initiatives.
- The Office for Prospective Students created "Wolf-Packed Fridays" to use a play on words for the campus Wolf mascot to enhance the tightly scheduled campus visit program with classroom experiences, tours of specific areas of interest, and academic sessions.
- The Gear Up program for Reno-area seventh through twelfth graders (by cohort) was initiated by Student Success Services as was middle school outreach in northern and southern Nevada.
- Two additional recruiters capable of working with diverse populations were hired into the Office for Prospective Students.
- Additional bilingual recruitment materials and materials for students with disabilities were developed by the Disability Resource Center.

- The diversity of the student staff throughout the Student Services division was increased to 35 percent students of color.
- The early advisement program (Wolf Pack Prep) was restructured by Academic Affairs and Student Services to be more comprehensive.
- Clear special admissions guidelines for all students with special talents were established by the Registrar.

2003 Goals

- The office for International Students and Scholars and Graduate School Admissions will relocate to the new student services building to best serve all students.
- The diversity recruitment plan with accountability measures will be implemented by the entire Division of Student Services.
- Partnerships with academic representatives will be expanded by the Office for Prospective Students through recruitment and early outreach efforts.
- Web-based recruitment efforts will be increased by the Office for Prospective Students for students from Nevada and out of state.

Theme Two: Retention and Persistence

We will improve the retention and persistence of all students through the development of programs that assist them at various stages in their higher education and that address the needs of specific groups. We recognize the importance of financial assistance and are committed to pursuing solutions to the lack of sufficient need-based aid, scholarships, and grants. The changing demographics in our student body require a staff that will become increasingly diverse as well as educated on the means necessary to create an intercultural campus climate.

Accomplishments. Accomplishments related to the KPIs for this theme include policy changes, reorganization, outreach, and enhancement of the academic experience:

- Admissions and Records policies now allow individual course withdrawals and refunds after the drop deadline. Davis grants for low income students are changed to retention and not recruitment incentives.
- The academic affairs/student services task force on retention was merged with the retention and persistence team, which adds four academic members to the team.
- Two grants were submitted by Student Services this fall. The McNair Scholars program would support a cohort of undergraduate students

of color in preparation for graduate school. The institutional enhancement grant to promote library research among millennium scholars was not funded.

- A six-month review by Enrollment Services of all financial assistance available to students resulted in revisions that stretched existing dollars further and created a well-researched request for the use of future funds through grant fund reallocations and private fundraising.
- Retention efforts led by Student Life Services like the Millennium Persistence Program and Rural Assistance Program were increasingly effective. Over 90 percent of the Millennium Scholars retained eligibility.
- An academic and career program counseling students on academic warning and probation was coordinated by Career Services and Academic Advisement.
- Campus services were developed by the Student Conduct Office to provide court referrals and appropriate interventions to students charged with alcohol violations.
- A peer education program was developed by Counseling and Student Conduct to change unhealthy behaviors around alcohol.

2003 Goals

- Student Life Services will develop venues to increase collaboration between academic affairs and student services, such as freshmen and sophomore centers, the Rural Assistance Program, and the millennium academic persistence program.
- Digital Initiatives and Student Services will design an e-brochure on retention topics and experts.
- Student Advocacy will develop the Freshmen Connections Program.
- Student Advocacy will establish a sophomore center.
- The Vice President of Student Services will create a seminar to address best practices in retention and persistence.
- The Vice President's Office will study and apply specific retention data on student cohorts as a basis for developing effective retention efforts.
- The Vice President's Office will consolidate assessment reports on campus retention programs.
- The Vice President's Office will pursue policy changes to revise the language for Millennium Scholarship and Davis Opportunity Grant eligibility from "twelve credits" to "full time" in order to allow students with disabilities to be eligible under the reduced course load policy.

Theme Three: Graduate Students

We will partner with others to create an exemplary graduate student experience, as well as provide programs and services to support a positive, progressive learning environment. We will seek affordable housing, on-line services, and scholarships. In addition, we will promote needed services to accommodate student evening and weekend schedules.

Accomplishments. Accomplishments related to the KPIs focus on attention to services, data accumulation, and review and affordable housing:

- A grid of services for graduate students campuswide was prepared by the Vice President's Office.
- A review of existing data on use of services by graduate students was conducted by Student Activities.
- Potential building of graduate/adult units was discussed by Residential Life with eight housing developers.
- A university rental property agreement with the GSA was signed, giving graduate students priority for university residential rental properties.
- A graduation ceremony for graduate students was created and successfully implemented by Enrollment Services.
- An admissions evaluator was moved from admissions and records to the graduate school to handle international graduate applicants.
- Temporary transitional housing arrangements were made by Student Advocacy with the University Inn Hotel for graduate students for January and August each year.
- Web pages for student services now include specific services for graduate students.
- The counseling center provided ongoing clinical training in collaboration with the university's academic departments.

2003 Goals

- The limited data available on graduate student use of services demonstrated a need for more assessment campuswide. The Strategic Implementation team will pursue this.
- Graduate housing that is affordable and close to campus still needs to be found by Student Services and Facilities Administration.
- Financial assistance needs to be secured and increased for graduate students through the combined efforts of Financial Aid, the Graduate School, and Development office.
- The GSA needs the assistance of Student Activities in finding a stable and increased funding source.

NEW DIRECTIONS FOR STUDENT SERVICES • DOI: 10.1002/ss

Theme Four: Residential Community

We will become a more residential campus by expanding our housing system and dining facilities. We will continue to offer a variety of well-maintained housing options to attract and retain both graduate and undergraduate students. Emphasis on the traditional college student will remain with increased attention to providing a home for graduates, families, and older students.

Accomplishments. Accomplishments related to this theme centered on expansion, cost-effective outsourcing, assessment, support for student learning, and diversity initiatives:

- Construction of a $20 million residence and dining facility was started by Residential Life in August 2002 and to be opened in August 2003. This will add 259 more beds to the current 1,500 and expand food services to accommodate future growth.
- Food services, housekeeping and maintenance, laundry facilities, telephones, and vending machines will be outsourced by Residential Life to keep costs low.
- A Residential Life review of computer lab use and the number of personal computers in the residence halls (84 percent of residents possess them) resulted in the conversion of the Nye Computer Lab to a meeting room for the Residence Hall Association.
- Student satisfaction and needs were assessed by Residential Life and Dining Services in an annual fall survey, and the results were applied to changes in food services, academic programs, and cultural events.
- A highly successful substance-free housing living option was implemented by Residential Life that resulted in an overall hall GPA above 3.0.
- Academic intervention programs by Residential Life and Academic Advising to encourage scholarly persistence for hall students with less than a 2.0 GPA were continued.
- The Chartwell's Scholarship Fund was established for residence hall students.
- Awareness of and sensitivity to our multicultural population was promoted by Residential Life and Dining Services through special events in the food services areas, diversity bulletin board program, staff training, and overall programming efforts.
- A highly trained and diverse live-in staff was maintained in the residence hall system.
- Students of color were 21.2 percent of the fall 2001 residence hall population.
- Students from southern Nevada were 41 percent of the residence hall population in fall 2001 and 39.2 percent in fall 2002.

New Directions for Student Services • DOI: 10.1002/ss

- On-campus assignments were made for all entering freshmen from outside the area by Residential Life.

2003 Goals

- Residential Life will open a new residence hall and dining facility for fall 2003.
- Residential Life will accommodate all full-time freshmen who request housing.
- Residential Life will achieve a high level of occupancy and meal plan participation.
- Residential Life will maintain University Village so that low-cost graduate, adult, and family housing is available to our students.

Theme Five: New Student Union Community

We will build a centrally located student union that meets the needs of students and other members of the university community. It will be a larger facility that will accommodate the future growth of the student body. As one of the most innovative student unions in the country, the new facility will enhance the recruitment and retention of students and faculty. It will provide a safe and welcoming environment for all members of our diverse community. The planning process will be a collaborative effort that reflects our values.

Accomplishments. The accomplishments for the New Student Union Community have been significant but also preliminary. A year ago when the Jot Travis Student Union's Phase One plan was submitted, no one dreamed that the new student union concept would come so far within one year. The accomplishments include:

- Support for a new union was secured by Student Services from around campus during the strategic planning process.
- The president's May 2002 Phase IV strategic plan included the creation of a new student union.
- The university's long-term capital improvement list authored by the President's Cabinet included the new student union.
- There was widespread involvement by faculty, staff, and students in collecting information about best practices in unions at other universities
- The Mid-Campus Master Plan led by the Provost has identified options for the location of the new student union. The current vision is an estimated $35 million union with approximately 228,000 square feet.

NEW DIRECTIONS FOR STUDENT SERVICES • DOI: 10.1002/ss

2003 Goals. These goals focus on key performance indicators established around research, finances, assessment, programming, and community development:

- An assessment priority by Student Services will bring in union architects and consultants to assess current and future trends and wants and needs of students and other members of the community, including alumni. Dialogue by the Student Union will continue with students of color and their advocates in the creation of a cultural center to serve students within the union.
- Student Union led research will focus on current trends in union construction, visit to campuses with exemplary unions, and a review of another Nevada campus, UNLV's fiscal arrangements, administrative time line, and plans to improve their student union.
- Financing plans will be pursued by Student Services and Finance & Administration, beginning with a history of the current union's funding including research on other union finance models, development of student fee options, and discussions with the development office.
- Student Services will continue to collaborate on programs that address diversity issues and to reach out to build community on campus.

Theme Six: Assessment

We are committed to creating a "climate of assessment" in Student Services so that we may provide the highest quality and most effective programs. We will systematically assess student use, needs, satisfaction and educational outcomes on an ongoing basis to insure continued improvement and effective use of resources. We will continue to provide assessment training and tools to staff along with the expectation that they will conduct and apply assessment.

Accomplishments. Accomplishments of the team focus on their mission to be a resource, to coordinate data collection, to educate the university about our students, and to promote the use of assessment as a critical component of databased decision-making:

- The strategic implementation team met consistently every other week and in doing so established a strong collaborative network that promotes assessment and its application throughout the division on an ongoing basis. Steve Cavote of the university's assessment office is an integral part of the team, and team chair Jacque Pistorello is on the university's assessment advisory committee. There is strong collaboration between this team and the university assessment office.

- Team members in the division successfully removed myths and stigmas around assessment through increased visibility and accessibility. In-person interviews with each department's assessment liaison in the division, making the team available to staff for assessment consultations, and follow-up with offices silent on assessment have moved our agenda along.
- The team created a concise baseline survey, posted on the Web site, for assessment liaisons in the division. It will be a gauge of attitudes, beliefs, and behavior regarding assessment, which will help team members bring about a cultural shift in how assessment is perceived.
- After the interviews of department assessment liaisons by team members, the entire team discussed a summary of findings.
- The Cooperative Institutional Research Program Freshmen Survey was conducted at new student orientation. Results will be available in early January 2003.
- An analysis of 2001 graduates was conducted by the team to determine if transfer students graduated at the same rate as native students.
- Nontraditional and transfer student assessment completed by the team clearly defines student transition needs now being built into programs and services.
- The substance abuse program implemented an assessment for students who violated alcohol policies, which results in appropriate intervention services.
- All student services departments have developed assessment plans for their services.

2003 Goals

- The team will guide the division through the use of results in affirming, revising, or eliminating programs and services.
- The team is currently designing a WebCT course for student services colleagues. The course will have links to useful assessment sites and summaries of assessment activities within the division and provide a forum for discussion on assessment activities.
- The June 2003 student services retreat will include a showcase of each department's assessment activities and the resulting impact of the assessment on programs and services.

Theme Seven: Technology

We are committed to integrating technological practices and advances into our programs and services for students. We will expand web-based services and improve use of technology to maximize its benefits. Each staff member will take advantage of the wide range of training programs to broaden their knowledge and skills so that they will be capable of enhancing services to our students.

Accomplishments. Key performance indicators and accomplishments regarding technology focused on the subthemes of Web-based services, staff training and development, and centralization of technology decision making:

- Student services Web sites were surveyed for compliance with the university's Web style guide and worked with those offices not in compliance.
- The results of a student Web usability study were applied to improvements.
- A student Web developer position was created by the Office of the Vice President to work with the campus Webmaster on developing and deploying templates for student services.
- Increased functionality through e-PAWS resulted in the elimination of paper notification to financial aid applicants. All students can access the Degree Audit Report reports, Web-registration transcripts, class schedules, and admissions file completion information on the Web.
- Student financial services collaborated with Student Computing Services to automatically create an SCS-generated e-mail account for all newly admitted students.
- Best practices in faculty and staff technology training and development programs were identified by the Vice President's office.
- Opportunities for student services personnel were created by the Vice President's office to assess their technological skills and receive training online.
- Until a position to coordinate such efforts is funded, each associate vice president will appoint a liaison responsible for communicating technology issues to the team.

2003 Goals

- The technology team will conduct a second student Web usability study, and apply the results to improvements.
- The Vice President of Student Services will form a Web development consultation group with the goal of providing students with uniformly high-quality, reliable information and service.
- In conjunction with the campus Webmaster, the student Web developer will create content management for the division.

New Directions for Student Services • DOI: 10.1002/ss

- Technology skills development will be included in the annual evaluation process.
- Identify student technology workers in the division, and understand their role in technology decision making and implementation. The team will develop a series of workshops for these workers to familiarize them with the campus information technology guidelines.
- The team will develop a strategy to hire a student services professional to coordinate a detailed plan for using technology in serving our students.
- The team will sponsor a technology summit for the division on February 27, 2003. It will focus on skills for optimizing technology in Student Services.

REFERENCES

Association of Public Land-Grant Universities. *Kellogg Commission Report on the Future of State and Land-Grant Universities.*Washington, D.C.: Association of Public Land-Grant Universities, 2001.

SHANNON E. ELLIS is vice president of student services and adjunct faculty in the College of Education at the University of Nevada, Reno.

NEW DIRECTIONS FOR STUDENT SERVICES • DOI: 10.1002/ss

INDEX

Statement of Ownership

Statement of Ownership, Management, and Circulation (required by 39 U.S.C. 3685), filed on OCTOBER 1, 2010 for NEW DIRECTIONS FOR STUDENT SERVICES (Publication No. 0164-7970), published Quarterly at Wiley Subscription Services, Inc., at Jossey-Bass, 989 Market St., San Francisco, CA 94103.

The names and complete mailing addresses of the Publisher, Editor, and Managing Editor are: Publisher, Wiley Subscription Services Inc., A Wiley Company at San Francisco, 989 Market St., San Francisco, CA 94103-1741; Editor, Elizabeth J. Whitt, Office of the Provost, Professor, Graduate Programs in Student Affairs, The University of Iowa, 111 Jessup Hall, Iowa City, IA 52242; Managing Editor, None.

NEW DIRECTIONS FOR STUDENT SERVICES is a publication owned by Wiley Subscription Services, Inc.. The known bondholders, mortgagees, and other security holders owning or holding 1% or more of total amount of bonds, mortgages, or other securities are (see list).

	Average No. Copies Each Issue During Preceding 12 Months	No. Copies of Single Issue Published Nearest To Filing Date (Summer 2010)
15a. Total number of copies (net press run)	1,031	906
15b. Legitimate paid and/or requested distribution (by mail and outside mail)		
15b(1). Individual paid/requested mail subscriptions stated on PS form 3541 (include direct written request from recipient, telemarketing, and Internet requests from recipient, paid subscriptions including nominal rate subscriptions, advertiser's proof copies, and exchange copies)	297	272
15b(2). Copies requested by employers for distribution to employees by name or position, stated on PS form 3541	0	0
15b(3). Sales through dealers and carriers, street vendors, counter sales, and other paid or requested distribution outside USPS	0	0
15b(4). Requested copies distributed by other mail classes through USPS	0	0
15c. Total paid and/or requested circulation (sum of 15b(1), (2), (3), and (4))	297	272
15d. Nonrequested distribution (by mail and outside mail)		
15d(1). Outside county nonrequested copies stated on PS form 3541	73	73
15d(2). In-county nonrequested copies stated on PS form 3541	0	0
15d(3). Nonrequested copies distributed through the USPS by other classes of mail	0	0
15d(4). Nonrequested copies distributed outside the mail	0	0
15e. Total nonrequested distribution (sum of 15d(1), (2), (3), and (4))	73	73
15f. Total distribution (sum of 15c and 15e)	370	345
15g. Copies not distributed	661	561
15h. Total (sum of 15f and 15g)	1,031	906
15i. Percent paid and/or requested circulation (15c divided by 15f times 100)	80.0%	78.9%

I certify that all information furnished on this form is true and complete. I understand that anyone who furnishes false or misleading information on this form or who omits material or information requested on this form may be subject to criminal sanctions (including fines and imprisonment) and/or civil sanctions (including civil penalties).

(signed) Susan E. Lewis, VP & Publisher-Periodicals

NEW DIRECTIONS FOR STUDENT SERVICES

ORDER FORM SUBSCRIPTION AND SINGLE ISSUES

DISCOUNTED BACK ISSUES:

Use this form to receive 20% off all back issues of *New Directions for Student Services*.
All single issues priced at **$23.20** (normally $29.00)

TITLE	ISSUE NO.	ISBN

Call 888-378-2537 or see mailing instructions below. When calling, mention the promotional code JBNND to receive your discount. For a complete list of issues, please visit www.josseybass.com/go/ndss

SUBSCRIPTIONS: (1 YEAR, 4 ISSUES)

☐ New Order   ☐ Renewal

U.S.	☐ Individual: $89	☐ Institutional: $259
CANADA/MEXICO	☐ Individual: $89	☐ Institutional: $299
ALL OTHERS	☐ Individual: $113	☐ Institutional: $333

Call 888-378-2537 or see mailing and pricing instructions below.
Online subscriptions are available at www.onlinelibrary.wiley.com

ORDER TOTALS:

Issue / Subscription Amount: $ _____

Shipping Amount: $ _____
(for single issues only – subscription prices include shipping)

Total Amount: $ _____

SHIPPING CHARGES:
First Item $5.00
Each Add'l Item $3.00

(No sales tax for U.S. subscriptions. Canadian residents, add GST for subscription orders. Individual rate subscriptions must be paid by personal check or credit card. Individual rate subscriptions may not be resold as library copies.)

BILLING & SHIPPING INFORMATION:

☐ **PAYMENT ENCLOSED:** *(U.S. check or money order only. All payments must be in U.S. dollars.)*

☐ **CREDIT CARD:**   ☐ VISA   ☐ MC   ☐ AMEX

Card number _____ Exp. Date _____

Card Holder Name _____ Card Issue # _____

Signature _____ Day Phone _____

☐ **BILL ME:** *(U.S. institutional orders only. Purchase order required.)*

Purchase order # _____
Federal Tax ID 13559302 • GST 89102-8052

Name _____

Address _____

Phone _____ E-mail _____

Copy or detach page and send to: **John Wiley & Sons, PTSC, 5th Floor**
                                     989 Market Street, San Francisco, CA 94103-1741
Order Form can also be faxed to: **888-481-2665**

PROMO JBNND